Designs on the Contemporary

Designs on the Contemporary

Anthropological Tests

PAUL RABINOW AND
ANTHONY STAVRIANAKIS

The University of Chicago Press
Chicago and London

Paul Rabinow is professor of anthropology at the University of California, Berkeley. He is the author or coauthor of many books, including *The Accompaniment* and *Designing Human Practices*, both published by the University of Chicago Press.
Anthony Stavrianakis received his PhD in anthropology at the University of California, Berkeley. Together they are coauthors of *Demands of the Day*, also published by the University of Chicago Press.

The University of Chicago Press, Chicago 60637
The University of Chicago Press, Ltd., London
© 2014 by The University of Chicago
All rights reserved. Published 2014.
Printed in the United States of America

23 22 21 20 19 18 17 16 15 14   1 2 3 4 5

ISBN-13: 978-0-226-13833-6 (cloth)
ISBN-13: 978-0-226-13847-3 (paper)
ISBN-13: 978-0-226-13850-3 (e-book)
DOI: 10.7208/chicago/9780226138503.001.0001

Library of Congress Cataloging-in-Publication Data

Rabinow, Paul, author.
   Designs on the contemporary : anthropological tests / Paul Rabinow and Anthony Stavrianakis.
       pages ; cm
   Includes bibliographical references and index.
   ISBN 978-0-226-13833-6 (cloth : alk. paper) — ISBN 978-0-226-13847-3 (pbk. : alk. paper) — ISBN 978-0-226-13850-3 (e-book) 1. Anthropology—Methodology. 2. Anthropolgy—Research.   I. Stavrianakis, Anthony, author. II. Title.
   GN33.R33 2014
   301.01—dc23

                                                        2013036400

♾ This paper meets the requirements of ANSI/NISO Z39.48-1992 (Permanence of Paper).

CONTENTS

Just as one can take up the "modern" as an ethos and not a period, one can take it up as a moving ratio. In that perspective, tradition and modernity are not opposed but paired: "tradition is a moving image of the past, opposed not to modernity but to alienation." The contemporary is a moving ratio of modernity, moving through the recent past and near future in a (nonlinear) space that gauges modernity as an ethos already becoming historical.

—Paul Rabinow[1]

What is an "anthropology of the contemporary"? It might well seem that the answer to this question was ready at hand given that Paul Rabinow had been using the term as a marked placeholder for quite some time.[2] In fact, some of its contours and some of its determinations have been established; they had been conceptualized and narrated in a series of books. Over the course of years, while other projects were under way, this preliminary labor consisted of inventorying elements and sketching topological parameters, as well as genealogically assaying components—each undertaken with a great deal of nominalist prudence. And yet, there was never any doubt that all of these laboriously achieved but jaggedly forged anthropological tools, or ideas for tools, were at best aspects of a still murky figure of the contemporary or, better yet, a contemporary. In any case, they remained to be assembled and tested for their coherence, as well as for whatever pragmatic payoffs in understanding and practice that they might provide, by bringing them into a functional proximity and observing how things ramified.

Designs on the Contemporary follows from and is informed and chastened by over five years of collaborative participant-observer-based inquiry. We have provided an account of that inquiry in our jointly written book

Demands of the Day: On the Logic of Anthropological Inquiry.[3] We analyzed there the logical elaboration of the conceptual and experiential steps required to reach the threshold of an anthropology of the contemporary properly speaking. After finishing *Demands of the Day,* and after a pause during which Stavrianakis spent a semester in Paris before returning to Berkeley during the summer of 2012 as a postdoctoral fellow in the Anthropology of the Contemporary Research Collaboratory (ARC), we considered the possibility of devising a project with a more traditional division of labor. We imagined the project centering on a problem articulated by Michel Foucault (but also in different manners by Max Weber and John Dewey and others yet to be named) of the modern severing of truth, subjectivity, and care. Initially, we divided the labor into two parts: while Rabinow proposed to take up the challenge of truth speaking in the last year of Foucault's lectures at the Collège de France, Stavrianakis was motivated to take up Foucault's rethinking of modes of subjectivation starting from the writings of Seneca. Foucault's emphasis on the motion of Stoic philosophy, we both agreed, seemed catalytic with respect to the task of thinking about motion in anthropological inquiry.

What began as a cooperative project soon morphed into a collaborative one in which we decided to write an essay or two together: in the fall of 2012, after a number of months of discussion, note taking, and preliminary formulations, we understood that we were in fact in the process of drafting another book together. Thus, we offer a collaboratively crafted essay that we trust begins to provide a warranted and vindicatory narrative of the requirements of a form for an anthropology of the contemporary.

As befits a preface, we underscore several markings that should help to indicate something about the topography of the contemporary as object, ethos, and form. First, the category of the contemporary is part of a series: present, actual, contemporary. We argue that one can only arrive at a specific form of a contemporary by working through a particular series of steps: there are no shortcuts. The anthropological work of diagnosing and giving form to an experience of participant-observation and then, and only then, delineating a logic of what we call the *actual* is a mandatory sequence (albeit an iterative one). We insist that for anthropology to be the kind of science that it ought to be, inquiry in John Dewey's sense of the term is demanded. That being said, and before multiple expressions of outrage are given voice, obviously what we intend by the term *anthropological science*—or *anthrōpos + logos*—is not the only kind of science available, desirable, or possible.

Second, both the objects and objectives (again, in Dewey's sense of these terms), as well as the mode of subjectivation of the anthropological inquirer, turn on a practice of form-giving rather than ideas, values, or symbols. That being said, clearly elements of the latter (ideas, values, symbols) may well figure as components of whatever form is being considered or constructed. Third, prior to, during, and after the process of inquiry, attention must be paid to what we call the *ethical substance* of the inquirer. Again many possible variants have been, are, and will be available. For us, the ethical substance of the kind of anthropology we deem worthwhile is one in which *truth* and *conduct* are brought into a form-giving relationship.

Fourth, we have concluded that a privileged site for conducting the anthropology of the contemporary is what Michel Foucault has called *foyers d'expérience* and which we call *crucibles of the contemporary*. Foucault identifies *foyer d'expérience* as venues in which

> forms of a possible knowledge (*savoir*), normative frameworks of behavior for individuals, and potential modes of existence for possible subjects are linked together.[4]

How this linking is possible, how it takes place, where it takes place, and under what conditions it takes place, are largely unexplored conceptually and logically, and no doubt these processes and venues are multiple and dynamic. In what follows, we will explore several instances of the dimensions and determinations of diverse crucibles of the contemporary.

Fifth, lurking at the margins of our project at its outset were two sets of distinctions that we felt to be important although for quite some time we were not sure why they seemed so salient. The first pair turned on Gilles Deleuze's claim that Foucault's oeuvre was riven throughout by two planes: "sayability" (*énonciabilité*) and "visibility" (*visibilité*).[5] One reason this distinction seemed illuminating for Rabinow concerned aspects of his prior reflections on Gerhard Richter, whom he had found intriguing but whose significance he could not pinpoint.[6] During the fall semester of 2012, Stavrianakis had become engaged with the "Rushdie affair" as raising complex anthropological quandaries. We thought including both Richter and Salman Rushdie as objects of a possible anthropology of the contemporary was a promising idea. Deleuze's distinction provided an initial scaffolding. How to think about Richter's insistence that his painting was about rendering visible something real that all of the ever-increasing body of art critics never seemed to quite identify? What was anthropological about Rushdie's struggles to find a form of written response to the fatwa issued by the

Iranians after the publication of *The Satanic Verses*? Our hope was that perhaps twining this pair of concepts and instances would illuminate not only key determinations of the contemporary but also provide tools for developing its anthropology.

Sixth, the second paired distinction—*Pathosformel* and *Nachleben*—we drew from the twentieth-century art historian Abby Warburg. Warburg worked against the grain of histories of art that narrated a progressive history arguing that older aspects lingered (*Nachleben*) and needed to be recognized and acknowledged as vital aspects of the artistic and human endeavor. Warburg was not rejecting the new per se, only insisting that older elements were at play. The stakes were not for or against historical change but rather were concerned with how old and new elements combined, or failed to combine, in artistic and ritual forms. Although we put them to a quite different use, Warburg's concept pair provides a way to approach the moving ratios of style and practice.

We claim that the instances we provide are contemporary ones in an anthropological sense, but we are under no illusions that what we offer here is comprehensive or definitive. Quite to the contrary, we offer what follows as stimuli, calls to others to engage in a practice that, at least for us, has been freeing from the *stultitia* and stasis of the already known, as well as from the vertigo of the merely speculative. We offer this work in the spirit of a patient impatience that opens the possibility of increasing our capacities without intensifying the ever-present debilitating relations—veridictional, jurisdictional, and subjectivational—that abound both within the academy and without. Finally, we hold out the hope that it might contribute to ways in which one might find a form in which to pursue *Wissenschaft als Beruf*, disciplined inquiry and thinking as a way of life, one form of *logos + anthrōpos*.

PART ONE

After the Actual

INTRODUCTION

The only possible anthropology is that where, rather than being tied to the passivity of phenomenal determinations, the Gemüt is instead animated by the work of ideas on the level of the field of experience.

—Michel Foucault, 1961[1]

Immanuel Kant taught his course on anthropology before, during, and after the publication of his critical philosophy.[2] Although it was a source of pleasure and income for the austere Kant, he considered the gathering up of customs and manners of the world's people of great significance in delimiting the practices and hopes of this distinctive creature. As is well known, during the 1980s Michel Foucault, toward the end of his life, took up Kant's punctual interventions as the site in which it seemed fruitful to reproblematize modernity, the Enlightenment, and their relations and interferences.[3] As is equally well known by now, in 1961 Foucault submitted his secondary doctoral thesis on Kant's *Anthropology from a Pragmatic Point of View*, translating it into French as well as providing a commentary.[4] Today, it is arguably the case that Kant's punctual writings never were nor are they now so minor after all.[5]

One could argue that Kant's insistence at the dawn of philosophic modernity that what others considered to be the banally empirical, the domain of the multiple and the heterogeneous, nonetheless constituted the site where indispensable curiosity could be satiated and surprising insights could be garnered concerning the contours of this peculiar being's habits and manners. Foucault, arguably at the waning of modernity's hegemony, or at least the nadir of its ascendency, returned to Kant in the hope of finding a form of and for Enlightenment in what he referred to as the *actual* (*l'actualité*).[6] This site of truth and conduct held uncanny echoes but also bitter reminders from Kant's reflections at the dawn of modernity on philosophy's tasks and obligations within the historical and political situation of the day.[7] Today, the challenge for us is how, once again, to inquire into, conceptualize, and give form to possible solutions to the contemporary reproblematization of truth and conduct.

The Problem of Modern *Anthrōpos*

In his *Introduction to Kant's Anthropology*, Foucault rethought Kant's text, investigating the relations of psychology (dispositional investigations of customs and manners of the savages) and anthropology to Kant's critical philosophy. The question Foucault began to articulate in 1961 was how it became not only possible but mandatory to engage in empirical analysis of the multiple practices of human beings, on the basis of an object of knowledge—"man"—simultaneously a natural creature conditioned by physical forces and a subject capable of freedom and intervention in the lived conditions of its own being.

Kant, in his *Anthropology from a Pragmatic Point of View*, distinguished between two forms of anthropological investigation (*Erforschung*), physiological and pragmatic:

> Physiological knowledge (*connaissance* / *kenntnis*) of the human being concerns the investigation of what nature makes of the human being; pragmatic, the investigation of what he as a free-acting being makes of himself, or can and should make of himself. . . . Such an anthropology, considered as knowledge of the world, which must come after our schooling, is actually not yet called pragmatic, when it contains an extensive knowledge of things in the world . . . but only when it contains knowledge of the human being as a citizen of the world.[8]

Foucault articulates precisely the significance and signification of anthropology as *Erforschung*:

> The initial objective of Anthropology is to be an *Erforschung*: an exploration of an ensemble never graspable in its totality, never at rest, because always taken up in a movement where nature and freedom are bound up in the *Gebrauch*—one of the meanings of which is given in the word "usage" (practices).[9]

The problem Kant articulated—the relation of "can" and "should" in the self-understanding of *anthrōpos*—is, we argue, being refigured today perhaps in diverse ways as possible solutions to a more general problematization.

Foucault underscored, however, that in Kant's *Anthropology*, the majority of the first part of the analysis does not in fact treat this object, the world citizen (*der Weltbürger*), in its cosmopolitical dimension, but rather, man as object "from the interior point of view of the *Gemüt*." It is by turning to *Gemüt* and not the world citizen, as telos of anthropological investigation, that we might be able to reproblematize Kant's anthropological problem. *Gemüt*

> includes the capacity to effect the unity of empirical apperception (*animus*) but not its substance (*anima*). *Gemüt* does not designate a substance (whether material or ideal) but is the position or place of the *Gemütskräfte* (the *Gemüt's* powers) of sensibility, imagination, understanding and reason.[10]

The *Gemüt* is the crucial topic because it is the site of self-affectation and the threshold of freedom. Kant tells us that "Spirit is the animating principle in the human being."[11] This animation is neither regulative nor determinative. It is of course not the motion or animation to be described by Hegel of *Geist* enveloping man and the world and then regulating the empirical diversity of the *Gemüt* in its historical determination and specificity.

Foucault writes of the function of *Geist* that it

> does not organize the *Gemüt* in such a way that it is made into a living be-ing, or into the analogon of organic life, or indeed into the life of the Ab-solute itself; rather its function is to visualize, to engender, in the passivity of the *Gemüt*, which is that of empirical determination, a teeming mass of ideas—the multiple structures of a totality in the process of becoming that make and unmake themselves like so many of the half-lives that live and die in the mind. Thus the *Gemüt* is not simply "what it is," but "what it makes of itself." And is this not precisely the area that the *Anthropology* defines as its field of investigation?[12]

If in Foucault's reading, the *Geist* is the animating principle of the work of ideas on the field of experience and self-affectation—the field of investigation for anthropology—two core *ideas* (in Kant's sense, concepts that go beyond experience and have their source in reason), which were animated with respect to what man can and should make of himself, and which became normative in anthropology as a twentieth-century discipline, were nature and culture.[13] In Kant's pragmatic sense, man is conditioned by both ideas. Kant states that

> all cultural progress, by means of which the human being advances his education, has the goal of applying this acquired knowledge and skill for the world's use. But the most important object in the world to which he can apply them is the human being: because the human being is his own final end.[14]

The pragmatic problem of *anthrōpos*, as a problem of natural law and cultural custom, is conceived by Kant in two steps. One way was in terms of the separation of knowledge of man as a natural thing, from man as a moral being. A second way was in terms of the problematic interdependence of knowledge of man and knowledge of nature, since man was considered to have a nature.[15]

The articulation of this problem was a development in how Kant conceived of anthropology relative to physical geography. He had been teaching physical geography from 1756 and anthropology from 1772 in Königsberg—the anthropology course became his most popular course and required a subscription fee, unlike the lectures on his *Critiques*, which were free and ill-attended. In 1797, with the French Revolution underway and conceding that he would not be able to teach his anthropology course again, because of his declining health, Kant agreed to have the anthropology lectures published; he clearly considered them to be an essential part of his overall corpus.

Foucault states that it was at this time that a shift can be seen in how Kant understood anthropological knowledge with respect to other kinds of knowledge of the world. As Foucault observes, what can be legitimately described as the dawn of a modern problem is as follows:

> Physical geography and anthropology are no longer set alongside one another as the two symmetrical halves of the knowledge of the world articulated on the basis of an opposition between man and nature. The task of directing us toward a *Weltkenntnis* is now the sole responsibility of an anthropology which *encounters* nature in no other form than that of an already habitable Earth (*Erde*).[16]

We accept the formulation that two separate forms of knowledge, one of *bios* and one of *anthrōpos*, is a problem. Today, however, the problem is compounded by a reversal of the hierarchy of knowledge from Kant's time: those claiming to produce knowledge of *bios* have gained political, financial, and institutional ascendency driven by the promise of health, prosperity, and comprehensive remediation. That this vision of a providential future comes equipped with an ever-receding horizon and with only man's insights and passions as its regulative idea is hard to contest. Although its actuality is available as knowledge to those practicing a pragmatic anthropology such knowledge does not overcome the disparateness and discordancy of the situation.

Furthermore, we hold that today the idea of a "habitable Earth" would have to be understood more in terms of a universal history and physical geography of an uninhabitable earth. Currently, the proposed form of *Weltkenntnis* is largely figural and falls, therefore, more in the realm of fiction, understood as operating on the register of the imaginary constructed with veridictional narratives, rather than the sovereign understanding of a totality that Kant hoped to see.

This state of affairs, this diagnosis in any case of our state of affairs, must confront what Foucault identifies as the "programmatic value" that Kant substituted for the cosmological:

> As a result, the notion of a cosmological perspective that would organize geography and anthropology in advance and by rights, serving as a single reference for both the knowledge of nature and of the knowledge of man, would have to be put to one side to make room for a cosmopolitical perspective with a programmatic value, in which the world is envisaged more as a republic to be built than a cosmos given in advance.[17]

We maintain that Kant's proposed horizons have not proven to be sustainable. The hope Kant held out for a *Universal History with Cosmopolitan Intent* guided by providence and leading to *Perpetual Peace* is barely intelligible today.[18]

How then to produce pragmatic anthropological knowledge? We hold that the pillars of the modern problem of pragmatic anthropological knowledge have been undone over the course of the last two centuries. Today we have serious doubts about the plausibility of a cosmopolitical horizon although we concur that it would be comforting to have available some general term to provide a unifying horizon beyond the particular and the singular.[19]

ONE

Problematization of the Modern: *Bios*

The only true anthropology is a pragmatic anthropology, where each fact is placed within the open system of können and sollen.

—Michel Foucault[1]

I continue to think that [we] require work on our limits, that is, a patient labor giving form to our impatience for liberty.

—Michel Foucault[2]

During 2006–2011 we undertook a series of experiments in collaboration among and between the biological and human sciences to see not only what we could (*können*) achieve by working together, but more importantly by seeking to ascertain what we should (*sollen*) achieve if things went as we hoped they would. That is to say, we wanted to see what would happen if a form of mutually enriching and synergistic practice could be imagined, invented, and experimented with, and its results analyzed. It is fair to say that when we began this project in 2006 we were working at the limits of what had been attempted previously by others within the prior jurisdictional forms to bring the biosciences and human sciences into a common frame in which actors contracted to a minimal equality, in the name of a vocational science worthy of the name.

We undertook these experiments as a task and an obligation. Consequently, as long as the work and its conclusions were rigorously and honestly carried out and iteratively evaluated, we would be satisfied that veridictionally our results, whatever they might be, would be warrantable and assertible.[3] At the end point of a five-year multisited and multi-investigator experiment, as well as concurrent sets of experiments in web-design and pedagogical innovation, we felt sure that the determinations produced within the *experimental systems* were pragmatically warrantable in the sense John Dewey has given to the term.[4] We had worked patiently attempting to invent forms and to occupy them; as we have documented, we encountered many obstacles in giving form to our impatience for a different practice of liberty, although we did succeed in practicing a form of *libertas*.[5]

Given the determinations we have established in, and from, our prior experimental situation, we were now in a position legitimately to put forth *judgments* as to what could be done currently within the framework of collaboration; and, in the light of the determinations that buttress those judgments, to propose a modified type of practice, a different manner of form-giving as to what is reasonable to hope for and to attempt today under actually existing conditions.[6] We were in a position, in other words, to pose the question: What difference does today make with respect to the near future?

In order to do so, however, in the light of our experiments and after sustained examination of the objects produced during the inquiry, we have found it necessary to reconsider, as well as to *reconfigure*, the core objects and determinations not only with which we had been engaged but more pertinent here with which we should now be engaged. Above all else, we have decided that we should and could concentrate on the forms, not just the ideas or values, which had always been the ultimate objective, we now came to realize, of the whole undertaking as well as the experiments in which we sought to put it to a test. We had begun with ideas (collaboration, practice, diagnosis, etc.) and values (trust, sincerity, truthfulness, etc.,), but no satisfactory forms. This lack was not a deficit as the whole undertaking was premised and contracted on the hoped for invention of new collaborative knowledge-seeking practices for the twenty-first century.

In this stage of evaluation, and as preparatory work to move ahead, the first crucial step was to reconsider what we had taken to be the problem space of our inquiry. Upon reflection, after having worked through as much as we had on multiple registers, we decided that the object and objective we had been actually assembling could be grouped under the term *bios*. Remembering that a term is a word + a concept + a referent, we began to understand more clearly that different and contrastive concepts and referents had been (and continued to be) collapsed under the same word.

Surprisingly, although some scholarly help concerning the term *bios* is available and some is invaluable in its own right; we discovered nonetheless that the existing inquiries and genealogies that have been produced so as to address objects and problems proximate to our own were in the end significantly different in their form and standards than ours such that their apparent proximity has proved to be an obstacle, at least initially, to our understanding and the invention of future form-giving.

Originally, we had been under the sway of our own assumptions that the core term (and its associated concepts and referents, as well as the problem space in which they were, had been and might be further situated) which we were striving to understand and to transform was *anthrōpos*. It was only after having brought to fruition a complex set of experiments in participant-observation, collaboration, and pedagogy, and equally having produced a series of books, that we came to appreciate that while *anthrōpos* unquestionably and self-evidently remains an objective for an anthropology of the contemporary; it apparently can only be arrived at after more mediations have been confronted, clarified, addressed, and worked through.

In that light, rather unexpectedly (and not without a certain obstinacy given how broadly these terms are taken to be as foundational ones which one cannot venture beyond) we had significantly less trouble concurring that neither *nature* nor *culture* had been either baseline terms or objects of inquiry for us. It was in that available light that it became clear to us that we had been working all along on *bios*. Such an insight was not exactly a surprise; we had been engaging with biologists all the way through and the whole enterprise had begun with a challenge to bring a branch of the postgenomic sciences into a productive relationship with an ethically informed anthropology.

Nonetheless, while in and of itself clarifying, identifying the term *bios* alone did not solve everything as recent decades have seen a proliferation of speculation on the term *life*. We had noticed during the course of our participant-observation that although the social sciences and a branch or two of high speculation in European philosophy had devoted themselves to deploying the term, we never encountered it as a technical term or object in an experimental system in the biosciences. There were thousands upon thousands of experiments concerning molecules; we had encountered none concerning the molecularization of life. In sum, *life* was not a scientific term—its concepts and referents were metaphysical or merely an exercise in proliferating *doxa*.

As to *life* in the social and philosophic discourses we knew rarely had been given a precise designation (in many cases because it was implied that its referent was to be found in the biosciences or in nature or in culture). When it has been given a more precise meaning and function, as in the work of Giorgio Agamben, we disagreed with the conceptual field and its associated claims. Agamben's sense of the term *life* as a problem space and an object enduring over millennia in Western thought and practice certainly did not harmonize with the work of Michel Foucault or Georges Canguilhem which we had a claim to understanding. Naturally that slippage, if slippage it were, did not invalidate Agamben's Heideggerian perspective but only indicated that the problem space and interpretive tools with which he had been laboring was significantly different from our own. We knew we had to construct a pathway different than Agamben's singular genealogy of life understood as a millennial reduction of *bios* to *zoe*, bare life.[7]

We also knew that parallel work was required to differentiate our inquiries from the sociological approaches perhaps most admirably developed by Nikolas Rose.[8] Rose's work was organized around the idea of *neoliberalism* and hence was primarily concerned with a mode of governance and secondarily with a mode of subjectivation (the responsible subject). Although Rose and his associates do take up veridictional concerns, they are consistently subsumed under and subsidiary to the jurisdictional and subjectivational modes. Like Agamben, although more historically and geographically delimited, Rose deploys the term *life* as a component of a neoliberal *world view*.[9] Taken in its own terms, the corpus of work constitutes a major contribution to understanding the present; its eschewal of conceptual work—"biopower is a perspective not a concept"—separates its objects, objectives, and ultimate goals from our own.

The Legitimacy of Modernity

This nature has nothing more in common with the ancient concept of nature to which the mimesis idea referred: the unmakable model of all that is made. That all phenomena can be manufactured is instead the universal presupposition of experimental investigations of nature, and hypotheses are outlines of instructions for the manufacture of phenomena. Nature then becomes the embodiment of the possible results of technology.

—Hans Blumenberg[10]

An important cornerstone of the ramifying conceptual architecture we are working within depends on the work of Hans Blumenberg. His diagnosis of the transformation of *nature* in modernity is a fundamental entry into a problem space that had no direct predecessors in the history of *ideas*. Following genealogical expositions of the present, Blumenberg could ground his admonition not to attempt to reoccupy the older problem spaces (cosmos, theology) in which nature had been located before modernity. With that illuminating insight, and within the constraints of his masterful and highly original history of ideas as responses to problems rooted in metaphors, Blumenberg, consistent with his own distinctive version of the history of the present, carried his explorations no further forward in time.[11]

Blumenberg's core enterprise was undertaken as a refutation not only of Heidegger's history of metaphysics about which Blumenberg frequently ironizes but more pointedly as a refutation of the position of Karl Löwith (and Carl Schmitt) that Western history should be seen as a long set of transformations of a unifying, underlying substance. Blumenberg devoted his intellectual efforts to reconceptualizing the history of ideas not as a set of transformations of a single theme but as a series of occupations and reoccupations of problem spaces. By so doing, he invented and carried out in extraordinary detail a set of genealogical exercises aimed at undermining and recasting the very idea of history as a progressive and unified unfolding.

Once this genealogical work was accomplished, once modernity was shown as a distinctive and unprecedented threshold event in the history of ideas, Blumenberg's persuasive diagnosis made itself available to be turned into a judgment. That judgment consisted in asserting, with all the genealogical warrantability he had made accessible, that the legitimacy of modernity consisted in leaving progressive philosophies of history behind, as well as those supposed universals, above all nature, which rather should be understood as reoccupations of a series of problem spaces. By refusing to reoccupy any slot in this series, Blumenberg provided a judgment as to what henceforth must be hoped for and undertaken: finding a vindicatory form for self-formation in thought.

In *The Legitimacy of the Modern Age* published in 1966, Blumenberg takes issue with Karl Löwith's central thesis from his 1949 work, *Meaning in History: The Theological Implications of the Philosophy of History*: that the idea of progress is an illegitimate secularization of a properly medieval and Christian conception of salvation. According to translator and Blumenberg scholar Robert Wallace, Löwith interprets eighteenth- and nineteenth-century philosophies of history

> as a "secularization" of the eschatological pattern set up by the Jewish and Christian religions, of their faith in a fulfillment of the world's history through "final" events.[12]

This eschatology is contrasted with ancient Greek philosophy and religion,

> founded on a "reverence for the past and the ever present," which are embodied in the cyclical pattern of reality exemplified by organic life and the revolutions of the heavens.[13]

For Löwith, the break in such cyclical understanding of reality was the introduction of

> novel ideas of creation from nothing and total final destruction, of a unique
> world history centered (in Christianity) on a unique Incarnation and directed
> at one absolutely final Judgment.[14]

Löwith claims that this is the single origin of the modern conception of progress.

Blumenberg's magnum opus, *The Legitimacy of the Modern Age*, contains a three-step response to the secularization thesis: (1) He offers an original and compelling alternative explanation for the sources of ideas of progress from the seventeenth century:

> The overcoming of the fixed authoritative status of Aristotelian science by the
> idea of a cooperative, long-term scientific progress guided by method; and
> the overcoming (in the literary and aesthetic realm) of the idea of ancient art
> and literature as permanently valid models of perfection in favor of the idea
> of the arts as embodying the creative spirit of their particular ages and in that
> sense capable of again achieving validity equal to that of the creations of the
> ancients.[15]

He then offers a caveat (2) that accounts for the complexity of the historical phenomena under discussion, in the transition out of "medieval ideas"

> there is a continuity of problems rather than of solutions, of questions rather
> than of answers.[16]

Blumenberg characterizes what is original about the overcoming of nature as a fixed system and permanently valid model of perfection, as "self-assertion." In his account, self-assertion is a response to a problem "posed for us by the overriding emphasis in the late Middle Ages on the theme of divine omnipotence."[17] As Blumenberg writes,

> The Middle Ages came to an end when within their spiritual system creation
> as "providence" ceased to be credible to man and the burden of self-assertion
> was therefore laid upon him. Thus "self-assertion" here does not mean the
> naked biological and economic preservation of the human organism by the
> means naturally available to it. It means an existential program, according to

which man posits his existence in a historical situation and indicates to himself how he is going to deal with the reality surrounding him and what use he will make of the possibilities that are open to him.[18]

The final move he makes is (3) that insofar as self-assertion is a response to a prior problem, a necessary acknowledgement so as to avoid the fiction of *de novo* developments in the history of ideas, nevertheless the specificity of modern ideas of "possible progress," a progress made possible by method and an open space of creation, was forced to

> reoccupy a "position" that was established by medieval Christianity, the "position" of an account of history as a whole.[19]

The refusal of such reoccupation is the means for a proper ethical understanding of the difference introduced by the development of *technē* in "nature." Nature here is a transformed concept and referent to the one referred to in ancient Greek philosophy: "the unmakable model of all that is made."[20] Rather, "nature," in a milieu of self-assertion, "becomes the embodiment of the possible results of technology."[21] An ethos has its correlates in *logoi* and *technē*. This has a striking consequence, which Blumenberg diagnoses very precisely:

> Only through the reduction of nature to its raw potential as matter and energy is a sphere of pure construction and synthesis possible. This results in a state of affairs that seems paradoxical at first glance: An era of the highest regard for science is at the same time an age of the decreasing significance of the object of scientific study.[22]

We thus see the increase in *technē* and *logoi*, within an appropriate modern ethos; however, within this modern ethos, we see that there has been little problematization of this decreasing significance correlative with the increase in specialized techniques and knowledge. Otherwise said, what have been and are the multiple possible responses to such a diagnosis of the modern?

Modern Pathos

As these [social] sciences have developed technically, the question of their moral status has become increasingly pressing. Yet, from a Deweyan point of view, most of the debates stimulated by this concern have been somewhat lacking in point, for they rarely have been based on any circumstantial examination of what such research is as a form of conduct.

—Clifford Geertz[23]

Anthropology has, during the course of the twentieth century, found itself at a series of junctures and impasses with respect to Blumenberg's diagnosis of the inverse relation of significance and technological progress. A central and important juncture point was the joint Harvard, MIT, and Ford Foundation projects of the 1950s, which sought to create interdisciplinary scientific interventions for development within modernization projects in newly emerging (postcolonial) states.[24]

In his 1968 "Thinking as a Moral Act," Clifford Geertz posed the question of the moral challenge characteristic of anthropological research at this juncture. Anthropology as a practice was—and still is—faced with the dual challenges of

the imbalance between the ability to uncover problems and the power to solve them, and the inherent moral tension between the investigator and his subject.[25]

With respect to the former aspect (problems), Geertz gives the example of the tradeoff and seeming inverse relationship between welfare and technological progress in Indonesia, and posed the question of their relation in Morocco:

One of the more *disquieting* conclusions to which thinking about the new states and their problems has led me is that such thinking is rather more effective in exposing the problems than it is in uncovering solutions for them. There is a diagnostic and a remedial side to our scientific concern with these societies, and the diagnostic seems, in the very nature of the case, to proceed infinitely faster than the remedial.[26]

Within a modernizing frame, prosperity, amelioration, and the flourishing of the researcher were not able to be coordinated.[27] Geertz, citing the French poet Alphonse de Lamartine, in his 1964 essay "Ideology as a Cultural System," wrote with regard to breakdowns in the new states that "the world has jumbled its categories"; the anthropologist looks on, patiently observing.

In the earlier essay, Geertz makes the case for how a science of ideology is possible with reference to the need to take into account symbolic forms. The anthropologist's task is the scientific study of the "three-dimensional process," of breakdowns in the Parsonian triumvirate of social reality, psychological mediation and the symbolic vehicles through which breakdown and mediation is expressed. What was not entertained was that Geertz's science could ever be inadequate or indeterminate with respect to the breakdowns that occasioned his thinking; what was not in question was the conduct appropriate to such indeterminacy. Geertz's scientific self-assurance was nevertheless qualified by his use of a subject term, *disquiet*, to characterize the scientific conclusions at which he had arrived.

The failure to produce a nonevaluative concept of ideology, in Geertz's assessment, stemmed from trying to handle the content of ideology, rather than to observe the symbolic webs in which ideological content is expressed. In the essay, he outlines two approaches to the study of social determinants of ideology, which exemplify such a limitation: interest theory and strain theory. The former is an analysis of the socio-economic interests of a rational actor, whose arguments are grounded in social structures. Geertz dismissed it as psychologically thin and sociologically muscular. The latter, by contrast, begins from a diagnosis of ideology as collections of political proposals that are responses to insoluble antinomies in social and psychological life:

> In the modern world, at least, most men live lives of patterned desperation. Ideological thought is then regarded as (one sort of response) to this desperation.[28]

Geertz's claim is that strain theory is diagnostically powerful but causally weak; the theory fails to show the relation between identified antinomies and action sanctioned, desired, or demanded. In Geertz's judgment strain theory lacks a concept of symbols, which mediate breakdown and action:

> The power of a metaphor derives precisely from the interplay between the discordant meanings it symbolically coerces into a unitary conceptual framework and from the degree to which that coercion is successful in overcoming the psychic resistance such semantic tension inevitably generates in anyone in a position to perceive it.[29]

Contrasting two metaphors, General Sherman's post–civil war statement "War is hell" and the Japanese military's 1934 statement "War is the father of creation and mother of culture," he writes of their status as meaningful claims about the world:

It is not the truth that varies with social, psychological, and cultural contexts
but the symbols we construct in our unequally effective attempts to grasp it.
War *is* hell and *not* the mother of culture, as the Japanese eventually discovered—although no doubt they express the fact in a grander idiom.[30]

Hence, Geertz can go on in the next sentence to write,

The sociology of knowledge should be called the sociology of meaning, for
what is socially determined is not the nature of conception but the vehicles
of conception.[31]

What is not in question is what we can claim about the world, but only
the "vehicles" through which people can claim what they claim about the
world. Geertz is defending a science of meaning, and not putting in question the meaning, or significance, of science.

Breakdown

What then to make of his later claim and call to examine research "as a form
of conduct"? Such examination is framed as part of an "inherent moral tension" between the anthropologist and those with whom he works in the
pursuit of the science of meaning. Geertz recounts such inherent tension
through a breakdown in a relationship with a key informant, stereotypi-
cally cast as a microethnographic episode. The breakdown turned on the
use of Geertz's typewriter, which he read as a symbolic vector of recognition
between himself and a local scholar, who had asked to borrow it. By borrowing the typewriter, Geertz claims that the local was asking to be taken
seriously as a writer, "by lending it I was tacitly granting that demand."[32]
As with his dismissal of reductive interest theory, he elevates the exchange
to a question of recognition, rather than see the exchange as a relation of
debt, credit, and power. In his own account, Geertz mishandled the situation by breaking the "suspension of disbelief," which was necessary for their
work together to continue.

Breakdown took the following turn in Geertz's story: concerned that the
borrowing had become more and more frequent and for longer periods
of time and concerned that he himself needed to use it, on a certain occasion he found an excuse to apologetically refuse the request to lend the
machine. This act was paralleled instantly on the part of the local writer by
way of an apologetic refusal to attend their next scheduled meeting. Until
this point the narrative of a game of recognition was still intact. As Geertz

narrates it, his shortcoming was the following: thinking he had made a fatal mistake to their ongoing relation, and concerned to repair it, he admitted in a roundabout way that in fact he had not needed the typewriter that day (the invented reason for the refusal) and that in fact the local writer could use it and he hoped he had not been offended. The narrative unraveled and the game was over; the writer responded that of course he had not been offended, it was after all Geertz's typewriter and that he was now too busy to ever meet again.

The lesson, it seemed for Geertz, was that his clumsiness had broken the rapport that would provide the means to observe the spinning of webs of signification. The suspension of disbelief was on Geertz's side, and hence he was the one to break it; his scientific orientation demanded that he read all situations as possible vectors of symbolic acts, rather than a situation of unequal power relations. Geertz was not inclined to read the situation in this way, for this would require the situation of breakdown, and the *conduct* of the inquiry itself to be taken up as part of the *scientific* problem for the inquiry.

Instead of breakdown and conduct appearing as part of the problem of inquiry, the two conducts of anthropology which Geertz names—diagnosis and fieldwork—are brought together through "disinterestedness":

> A partial achievement laboriously earned and precariously maintained. What *little disinterestedness* one manages to attain comes not from failing to have emotions or neglecting to perceive them in others, nor yet from sealing oneself into a moral vacuum. It comes from a personal subjection to a vocational ethic.[33]

What is not entertained is that the mode of subjectivation of his science could be inadequate to the breakdowns that occasion his thinking, and hence of what could be warranted about the objects of inquiry:

> Science names the structure of situations in such a way that the attitude contained toward them is one of disinterestedness . . . where science is the diagnostic, the critical dimension of culture, ideology is the justificatory, the apologetic one—it refers to that part of culture which is actively concerned with the establishment of patterns of belief and value.[34]

Culture as the object of inquiry in Geertz's science, operates as a justification of "disinterestedness" as the appropriate scientific position for observation and inquiry into breakdowns.

One could of course reverse this: disinterestedness, for Geertz, as an unchanging subjectivational mode assures the one who wishes to know that the object of knowledge does not need to change or be transformed. If Others have cultures, which produce webs of signification for dealing with breakdown, then the task for an anthropologist is to observe and describe those webs. If Others were not to have cultures that succeed in remediating breakdowns, then the anthropologist would have to start without knowing already what the object is, asking how the situation of breakdown is breaking down for both himself and those people with whom he is engaged. Geertz himself wrote,

> An attitude at once critical and apologetic toward the same situation is no intrinsic contradiction in terms (however often it may in fact turn out to be an empirical one) but a sign of a certain level of intellectual sophistication.[35]

The open question is what the inquirer is critiquing and then capable of warranting. Such a complex attitude seems to be both a problem and a task for an anthropological science capable of coming to terms with its own conditions of production. Geertz gestured toward, but did not pursue, the problem of how anthropology should come to terms with its modes of judgment, whose subjectivational dimension he names and restricts to "disinterestedness." Disinterestedness may be an element of warranted anthropological inquiry, but we are questioning whether it is sufficient for the subjectivational, veridictional, and jurisdictional demands for coming to terms with breakdowns in the motion of anthropological inquiry.

What is missing from Geertz's account is precisely an analysis of the excesses and deficiencies, and hence of the ethical mean, of anthropological participant-observation, as well of those with whom the anthropologist engages. In Geertz's portrayal "ethics," or taking up thinking as a moral act, is a methodological caution in the service of disinterested knowing. Ethics is thus on the side of the mode of the production of textual objects, which themselves can render present the semiotic webs of the Other. Ethics, in his account is not a constitutive part of what is to be known.

Dewey, in contradistinction to Geertz, and as we will take up in chapter two, claims inquiry begins with naming the structure of a situation as discordant. Situations of thinking do not preexist breakdowns which occasion thinking. Such discord, or breakdown in understanding, as well as the possible means of reconstruction or remediation, is thus not located unilaterally on the side of the Other. Situations hence pose the question of the appropriate attitude, standard, and forms for thinking about them.

The Problem Space of Truth and Seriousness: Occupy

In his 1983 essay "Humanism as Nihilism: The Bracketing of Truth and Seriousness in American Cultural Anthropology," Rabinow asked, why, given anthropology's traditional reflection on the Other as the object of inquiry, has anthropology not escaped the leveling of meaningful differentiation, which is the definition of nihilism? How, in other words, can anthropology take ethics seriously? This challenge was diagnosed as the result of a double bracketing with respect to the object of inquiry. The first bracketing was the result of the shift in object from "man" to "culture." To posit such objects, cultures, required the bracketing of truth. The truth of the existence of many cultures required a relativism of the truth content of those cultures. This prior truth is posited as an underlying universal boundary condition.[36] The content of these boundaries can then be positioned relative to one another.

The second bracketing was the result of a further transformation in the object of anthropological inquiry. With respect to key figures such as Geertz, Rabinow diagnosed the shift in object as turning on the reintroduction of historicity and symbols, a reoccupation resulting from the first bracketing in American anthropology.

Symbolic anthropologists, such as Geertz, argued against a conception of underlying universal boundary conditions, which were seen by such anthropologists as unspecifiable. In the place of this content-less universal condition, the human being was placed within a developmental (but not evolutionary) account of the role of culture in the development of the human thing.[37] The cultural character of human action, for a symbolic anthropologist, became irreducible to any underlying universals. The way to analyze cultures was thus through their symbols, which are concrete embodiments of ideas and judgments, and complexes of symbols are extrinsic sources of information. As such, the anthropological task was one of the translation of such symbolically constituted actions into the language of anthropology.[38] The second bracketing in American anthropology was thus of the seriousness of such symbols, which could be posited for the Other but only insofar as they are serious for them within their culture.

Rabinow's diagnosis was part of a broader effort in the 1980s to think through morality as a problem for the social sciences. The paper itself came out of an interdisciplinary conference organized in March 1980 at Berkeley, in part around the occasion of Jürgen Habermas's visit in the Winter Semester. Richard Rorty, Robert Bellah, and a range of philosophers, historians, and social scientists began discussions from two mutually implicated starting points, one that they shared with Geertz and another that they did not.

The shared diagnostic starting point was that modernization efforts of the 1960s (part of the "American Century") and the social sciences' role within that project were ultimately unsuccessful in their own terms. The diagnostic starting point through which Rorty, Bellah, and others differed was that value neutrality in inquiry is an impossibility and that there is not an adequate understanding of morality as both an object and component of the practice of social science inquiry.

The range of papers in the conference offered multiple differing responses to a double critique, of both positivism and hermeneutics, as failing to provide ethical warrant for the pursuit and practice of social science. Positivism, one could say following Blumenberg, illegitimately reoccupied a self-justified position of science and the scientist as bringing about the good and the right.[39] Hermeneutics as one possible response, however, was diagnosed as inadequate insofar as the

> desire to interpret a culture from within its own categories gives us no standard for evaluation. . . . When pressed to the extreme the interpretive enterprise can become as closed and self-satisfied as any scientific one. Our insistent problem then of the relation of social science to ethics is not solved by replacing one method with another.[40]

The trenchant diagnosis, which the human sciences have yet to squarely deal with, is that these methods do not contain their own ethical justification. Such self-contained ethical justification was given in philosophies of history as one means of underpinning both positivism and hermeneutics. Without a philosophy of history, ethical assurance falls away. How then to bring inquiry and conduct together without succumbing to either illusion about the goods of such work, or without abandoning the question of the ethical worth of inquiry for the one pursuing the inquiry?

Pierre Boudieu's preface to the French edition of Rabinow's *Reflections on Fieldwork in Morocco* intervenes, in part, on this question. On the one hand he praises the scientific act of taking as the object of an anthropological study, the study of fieldwork itself. There is in this move an objectification of the knowing subject, a subject not reduced to a "registering device." Bourdieu, however, offers a caution:

> Does not the relationship of inquiry itself, by creating a situation of theoretical interrogation in which the interrogated interrogates himself on that which

until then was unproblematic and self-evident, create an essential alteration, one capable of introducing a bias in all other observations collected that is more dramatic than all the distortions of ethnocentrism?

Bourdieu, it seems, is asking two interconnected questions: Where is breakdown located? (And as a consequence, what counts as a problem?) Who is the interrogated? For Geertz it could only be the Other, both as the interrogated and the site of breakdown.[41] The core question for Geertz was how symbolic forms governed social life. Participants in the 1980 workshop were actively trying to diagnose where breakdown could be identified and to reproblematize both culture and *anthrōpos* as objects of inquiry.

Writing Culture: A Blockage Point

A different effort to occupy the problem-space of culture was the 1984 Sante Fe Seminar, which resulted in the edited volume *Writing Culture*. The seminar's aim, according to the organizers James Clifford and George Marcus, was to specify how texts have been constructed in anthropology, how attention to textuality could change the manner in which texts are written, and through this attention begin to address the politics as well as poetics of ethnography. With respect to the purposes of the seminar, and with respect to our diagnostic concern of truth, conduct and anthropology, Clifford asked in his introductory essay,

> Where do "problems" come from? . . . Cultures are not scientific "objects" (assuming such things exist, even in the natural sciences). Culture and our views of "it," are produced historically, and are actively contested.[42]

Writing Cultures' overall contextualizing move was forceful in highlighting subjectivational and jurisdictional dimensions in how "our views" of "culture" take shape. The volume sidelined, however, the question of how veridictional, subjectivational, and jurisdictional vectors coalesce. The problem of social science as moral inquiry was not sustained or built on.

As both a text and a moment in the history of anthropology *Writing Culture* was a political response to the reoccupation of the problematization of culture. Such a reoccupation was a blockage to building on the themes of the Berkeley seminar. Furthermore, it is worth observing that *Writing Culture* as a text came out of a one-week seminar, after which the editors were able to rearticulate its core concerns through a diverse set of academic networks, journals, etc. What it lacked as a disciplinary intervention was the creation of further venues for reproblematization. Such a disciplinary remediation was attempted in Berkeley with Robert Bellah leading a collaborative group of social scientists who conducted inquiry into the moral problems of social life in contemporary America, published as *Habits of the Hearts: Individualism and Commitment in American Life.*[43]

Instead of a general movement toward producing venues for collaborative work on the relation of social science to questions of ethics and truth, following the model of Bellah and others, the trend was rather in the opposite direction: a mode of subjectivation was gradually rendered normative that anthropologists can speak neither *for* nor *about* their object of inquiry and this norm was then governed by formal and informal channels. This was reproduced on the object side of inquiry with modes of subjectivation coming to reoccupy the place of culture as object of inquiry. This had the positive ramification that objects of anthropological inquiry began to proliferate.[44]

Such a reoccupation, however, evaded the question of truth and subjectivity, of ethics in relation to the pursuit of social scientific inquiry, and of how venues for work on problematizations could be crucial to the work of reproblematization. Following Blumenberg we could say that to inquire into culture, or into modes of subjectivation per se is part of a "reoccupation" of a problem space; one which was an appropriate response to problems of the early twentieth century, but no longer appropriate to the heterogeneity of *logoi* and their proliferating objects, as well as the multiplication of turbulent discordancies on all sides, in the twenty-first. The challenge is to identify different problems, and venues for working on problems, which we can occupy.

Venues for the Problem of Bios

Through more than five years of experimentation in collaboration, we have determined that a necessary if not sufficient component in the invention of practices of inquiry is the venue in which it is pursued. The venue for inquiry is nonisomorphic with the physical spaces in which collaborative work occurs. In a venue for inquiry, thinking and writing, diverse factors and purposes are mobilized within a physical space. The available norms, forms, and standards will alter as the objects and objectives of thinking shift. We recognize that working through the problem spaces of nature and culture, toward that of *bios*, meant we should also ask which factors from prior venues for work on nature and culture, and ideas and values, we should take with us for our work on *bios* and forms.

Blumenberg had successfully used his venue—the lone researcher in his study with a long-term methodical plan and a mode of subjectivation to produce the discipline necessary to systematically carry out this plan—to identify and elaborate a history of problem spaces and ideas. We took two factors from Blumenberg and his mode of working: what to do with nature is a modern problem, which reoccupation of prior spaces will not only not solve, but will mislead; additionally, staying on the plane of ideas, given the validity of that prior claim and Blumenberg's masterly use of it was structured so as to go back in historical time. Thus, as admirable as Blumenberg's oeuvre is, it could only provide a diagnostic of problem spaces, their occupation, reoccupation, and nonoccupation.

Geertz had made advances in his venue—fieldwork, a comfortable study, writerly texts, prestigious academic appointments—of values and symbolic forms. We took factors from Geertz and his mode of working on culture as a modern problem: his diagnosis of the discrepancy between the ability to name problems and to provide solutions led to an impasse when values are the key factor. Just as Blumenberg's emphasis on ideas reached its limits for those searching for forms appropriate to a near future, so too Geertz's emphasis on values led to an antinomy for those searching for practices relevant for a near future. We drew from these observations that values should not be made the key factor. Values and symbolic forms are linked in the neo-Kantian approach since they both come from the subject, transcendental or pragmatic. Hence Geertz and his informant both had subject positions that could not be wished away. We drew from this the factor that communication and value mediation were not the path forward. What Geertz was really talking about was the form of their relationship.

Given the historical ontological status of nature and culture and their modern problematization, it seemed clear to us that these spaces were not the ones in which we wanted to operate. It also became clear that we had been interested in and concerned about *bios* all the way through and not nature or culture. The challenge of how to occupy the current problem space of *bios* turns, we have concluded, at least in part, on a refusal of the reoccupation of the problem spaces of nature and culture. Given that determination, the test was how to provide a form for *bios*? Such work entailed analytic breakdown of prior problem spaces and their reassemblage in a manner that diagnostically seemed appropriate to the task at hand.

Where did we do this ordering? We had a prior venue that had been successfully invented for working out of and through the experience of fieldwork and its aftermath.[45] We had come to understand that this venue for collaborative anthropology needed to be revisited, reexamined, and reassembled at each juncture as a different kind of work was undertaken. We needed to repurpose our equipment with respect to the problem we had identified. As we have written about previously, we used a web-based tool, the studio, as equipment through which to assemble experiences and the logical means for working through those experiences.

We drew from these determinations regarding venues, that in order to refashion the practices of *bios*, beyond the actual, we needed to return to our *venue atelier* for refactoring and repurposing. We brought the above factors into the existing venue so as to experiment with whether or not they could be repurposed. The factors we brought forward from Blumenberg and Geertz into our venue enabled us to know that we were not working on nature and culture, and that we should be finding a different mode of addressing the problem of *bios* in the near future.

One of the key functions of a *venue atelier* is to develop and test equipment on how to relate experience and logic. It facilitates the back and forth motion between writing together, experimenting with the available equipment as an initial objectification and testing ground, and the sorting out of experiential sequences and logical order.

The *venue atelier* enabled us each time to ask the historical ontological question, what is it that we are talking about? To raise the question of what objects are available for curating, refactoring, repurposing, and the objective question about the direction in which to proceed. All of these questions at each stage were directed at, and depended on, the status of appropriate practice, but that status could only be identified and rectified once this other work took place in the *venue atelier*. We found resources for our atelier in the philosophic fragments from the work site (*chantier*) of Foucault's explorations of the problem of *bios*.[46]

Technē tou biou: *Techniques of Self-Formation*

In October 1980, Foucault gave the Howison lectures at Berkeley under the title "Truth and Subjectivity." One can see in the distance and change from the Tanner lectures at Stanford in October 1979 (an investigation of pastoral power and modern political reason) motion toward a different problematization of knowledge, ethics, and power.[47]

Through his lectures at the Collège de France, in the volumes of the history of sexuality he was writing, and through a series of productive working relationships in the US, especially at Berkeley, Foucault thematized problems which centered on the interrelation of techniques, knowledge, and care within transformations of practices of the self. His working sessions with Rabinow and Hubert Dreyfus published as "On the Genealogy of Ethics" clarifies that the general ancient Greek problem was not primarily the self, or subject, but rather *technē tou biou*; the question of how to live, which gradually came to be subsumed within techniques and practices of the self.[48]

During this period Foucault opened up several paths for inquiry one of which was a diagnostically catalytic problem of how the question of the *technē tou biou*, the question of how to give form to one's existence, increasingly came to be posed in terms of how a subject must transform himself, so as to have access to the truth. Foucault's return to the period between fourth century BC and first century AD, from Socrates to Seneca, was a return to a moment in which he observed the problem of *bios* being tied to practices of the self. There was a reproblematization of *bios* in which the key shift was from a question of how a subject should live so as to rule the city toward a question of how he should live so as to care for himself.

The problem of *bios*, as a question of the care of the self, led Foucault to trace a path through which this problem was connected to truth telling as a practice. At several points between 1982 and 1984, he rearticulated his diagnosis of the separation of truth and care in modernity. A note in his manuscript for his 1982–83 lectures reads,

> This is why, finally, Western philosophy can be read throughout its history as the slow disengagement of the question: how, on what conditions can one think the truth? from the question: how, at what costs, in accordance with what procedure must the subject's mode of being be changed for him to have access to the truth?[49]

This means to truth, by way of knowledge alone, was institutionalized, organized, and regularized by the mid-nineteenth century. Within the sciences, the means to truth by way of knowledge were regularized by the structure of the object to be known, as well as through the rules of method and through the emergence of norms of research.[50]

Foucault, echoing Weber's 1917 diagnosis, claimed that with the separation of truth and care, and with the creation of fixed standards and forms of knowledge as the means to truth, knowledge

> will simply open out onto the indefinite dimension of progress, the end of which is unknown and the advantage of which will only ever be realized in the course of history by the institutional accumulation of bodies of knowledge, or the psychological or social benefits to be had from having discovered

the truth after having taken such pains to do so. As such, henceforth the truth cannot save the subject.[51]

Weber, following Tolstoy, characterized the question of the *technē tou biou* as the only question that counts and posed the question: In what manner does normed, structured, regularized science give "no" answers to the challenge of giving form to one's life? How if at all can normed, regularized practices of truth be connected to the conduct of a life that make the search for truth possible? Science, Weber tells us, may still be of use in posing the question.

Logic

No science, no *logos* can answer the question of how to live. The proliferation of reasoned discourses, about *anthrōpos*, nature, culture, history, and *bios*, have produced incompatible claims about their objects; few such discourses come with attendant reflection on practices and on conduct.[52] Once one recognizes that these hetero-*logoi* give "no" answers, at least *bios* as an object and problem is opened to further reflection and a search for appropriate and selected standards and forms. In this logic of thinking one must come to terms with the problem (indeterminations and breakdowns) of conduct in the face of proliferating *logoi* about *bios* and *anthrōpos* (and culture and nature). This mode of subjectivation must acknowledge the necessity of both separation and connection to the truth claims of sciences, as the path by which critical limitations can be named in a veridictional mode. Only then can the problem be reposed as conduct in the face of hetero-*logoi*.

What judgments can we make about the available forms for living, when we recognize the limits of all *logoi* to answer in a general and stable way questions of significance? This, we think, is the contemporary problematization of *bios*.

TWO

Logic

In Dewey's view, it is judgments, not propositions, which are warrantably assert-
able or not; and judgments are essentially rooted in concrete actions in the world
insofar as the consequences of such actions serve to decide their warrantability.

—Tom Burke[1]

Logic is not a method, but a moving series of standards and forms that
are demanded during the unfolding process of inquiry. Hence, at each moment or stage one is obliged to invent (in the older sense of the term) the
appropriate progression for that which one has already experienced, or for
that which one is doing the work in order to begin experiencing. Logic, either before or after one set of experiences, provides a conceptual ordering.
Within this dialectic or dynamic of logic and experience, there are moments
of confirmation or disconfirmation—an initial exercise of verification as to
the progress of the experiment. This process of verification informs one's
evaluation as to whether and where to proceed.

At this point in our reflections, we realized we were in a position to
ask how to give form to *bios* as a contemporary problem.[2] But more work
needed to be done before we could pose the forms and standards of that
step correctly. Our first step was to further explicate and test the adapted
logic, which we take from Dewey and through which we had previously succeeded in finding appropriate standards and forms for our inquiry.

The John Dewey scholar Thomas Burke notes that Dewey's use of the
term *situation* has been criticized by numbers of commentators as being
vague or underspecified. Given that this criticism is plausible, it is helpful to
see in the following quotes from Burke that two substitute terms for *situation*
are available—*instance* and *episode*. Burke observes:

Situations, occurring in the ongoing activities of some given organism/environmental system, are instances or episodes (or "fields") of disequilibrium, instability, imbalance, disintegration, disturbance, dysfunction, breakdown, etc.).[3]

Central to this process (the naming of which is itself secondary although not irrelevant) is the identification of ongoing activity, an encounter of a breakdown of some sort and the subsequent action of thinking in Dewey's sense, an activity that leads in some cases to inquiry in a more specific sense of the term:

> *Situations*, then, occur as instances or episodes of breakdown or imbalance in this dynamic integration.[4]

Situations, instances, and episodes then, we would say, occur in the *present*.[5] This claim needs to be nuanced, however, insofar as the types of instances that concern and interest us are probably generally already mediated conceptually to one degree or another. No doubt there are many types of such mediations in the world, including cultural ones, whose hub is not veridictional per se. As concerns an anthropology of the contemporary, however, it is those instances where we can prime veridictional concerns (almost certainly in a second-order observational mode) that impress themselves upon the anthropologist.

Propositions: Instrumentalities within Inquiry

Dewey's use of the term *inquiry* has proved extremely helpful in its conceptual elaboration of the steps and moments as a situational response to instances or episodes of breakdown, existential or otherwise. Furthermore, the term has proved useful as a comprehensive and transformative substitute for the term *method*. How to proceed in an experiment, as well as how to know if one is understanding what is happening during the immediate experiences of the experiment as well as its ramifications, conceptual and otherwise, has been a process that has been subsumed (and obfuscated) in recent centuries by the term *method*.

Dewey offers the most compelling available alternative for an engaged, active, and occasion-centered practice—one in which claims to serious speech acts can be made and, to use Dewey's technical language, *warranted*. Each and everyone one of the terms in the title of Dewey's book *Essays in Experimental Logic* is relevant and salient to recasting the process of inquiry.

Strikingly enough, the terms and distinctions of Dewey's recasting of inquiry (now a century old) is especially salient to the practice of anthropology in the twenty-first century.[6]

In previous work—especially *Demands of the Day*—we have attempted to provide at least some of the transformations that would be required to take Dewey's ultimately still philosophical (in the disciplinary sense) conceptual apparatus and to demonstrate how it might work both during and subsequent to an instance and case of actual (*sic*) inquiry in an anthropological mode.[7]

There are a series of more technical issues that Dewey addresses in his 1938 *Logic* and which have been given increased clarity and elaboration in Tom Burke's book, *Dewey's New Logic: A Reply to Russell*. Although Burke is himself a philosophic commentator and does not actually pursue an inquiry in any sustained way in the book, his explanations and clarifications now seem extremely helpful in addressing a series of insufficiently confronted issues in our own previous work. These issues turn on what we have come to call the practice of inquiry in which *truth* and *conduct* (to use two older terms that will have to be modified) are in a joined and mutually capacity-building relation. We use the term *parastēma* first introduced to us by Michel Foucault, whose passing references to Marcus Aurelius have turned out to be enlightening, clearing the way for more thought.[8]

What that relation (or relations) between *truth* (variously understood) and *conduct* (equally various) is—or can be or has been, or should be—turns on the question of form. Initially, the question of form here is a question of practice. Subsequently, it probably is a question of curation, then narrative and then *parastēma*.[9] The series is completed by challenges of intervention in a contemporary mode. Should anyone have the courage and endurance to traverse such a series, with any luck, new instances will be encountered, ones that might otherwise have passed imperceptibly by or ones for which the necessary equipment was lacking or insufficient.

The distinction Dewey draws between *propositions* and *judgments*, while technical nonetheless, has proved to be extremely pertinent for us in forging the equipment to identify and proceed toward a range of *pragmatic reductions* (of experience) through which an inquiry can be formed, be advanced, and transformed. Burke presents and clarifies the distinction between propositions and judgments in a series of steps. The first distinction underscores the kind or type of thing these terms refer to in Dewey's logic:

> Strictly speaking, it is not usually appropriate in Dewey's view to talk about
> the truth or falsity of propositions. Rather, propositions in a given context

are said to be *affirmed or denied* (or neither, or both), on the grounds of their being confirmed or disconfirmed, being relevant or irrelevant, informative or uninformative, effective or ineffective, consistent or inconsistent, useful or not, and so forth.[10]

As Burke discusses at length, Dewey's manner of drawing this distinction is a dramatic and provocative reversal of the standard use of the terms in modern logic from Frege to Russell. The reversal turns on Dewey's claim or insight that there are no facts (atomic or otherwise) lying out there in the world waiting to be captured by propositions. Facts emerge during inquiry; such a claim is pragmatic and realist in a direct sense and carries with it none of the constructivist or deconstructivist baggage that has come to fill late modern discursive space.

Burke argues that Dewey is not attempting to introduce a constructivist or solipsistic mode of inquiry but rather he is attempting to avoid the metaphysical position that rests on the world being a certain way. Propositions for Dewey are the kinds of speech acts that one affirms or denies (or both) on the basis of (and during the course of) ongoing inquiry:

> The notion of affirmation, unlike truth, is, among other things, verificationist in character. But this amounts to a claim about what propositions are, constituting not a verificationist theory of truth but rather a verificationist theory of propositions.[11]

Furthermore, the reason to conduct an inquiry (or to think) is not ultimately to affirm or deny (or both) propositions. For Burke, according to the view of

> any thoroughgoing empiricist—*things and events* are the material and objects of inquiry, and propositions are *means* in inquiry, so that as conclusions of a given inquiry they become means of carrying on further inquiries. Like other means they are modified and improved in the course of use.[12]

Propositions therefore can be understood as *intellectual instrumentalities*, to use Dewey's terms, which both arise within inquiry, provide a means to continue to verify the motion of the inquiry and provide equipment through which the *veridictional* register of an essay in experimental logic can be tempered.

For Dewey, propositions are what he has called elsewhere *intellectual instrumentalities*. They are the *means* by which the subject matter of an inquiry is described and subsequently made determinate.

We have discovered and confirmed that such determinations have a precise function. Burke phrases this point as follows: propositions, he posits that Dewey argues, have a

> "validity value" (to coin a phrase) as means to instituting warrantable assertable judgments. This involves not truth values but things like relevance, salience, coherence with other propositions, persistence in the face of ongoing inquiry (i.e. failing to be disconfirmed by ongoing experience), and so forth. There are existential factors which an inquirer has a direct handle on, whereas "truth" is a metaphysical idealization about which one too often can only speculate.[13]

Determinations thus are the content of one logical stage of inquiry given the form of propositions (terms) that can be affirmed or denied (or both). This process establishes them as a form of midrange or midprocess instrumentality that has been tempered and tested to a degree but which are not the ultimate goal of inquiry. To understand this claim we need to follow Dewey (and Burke) in their exposition of the term *judgments*.

Judgments

> A judgment, which is not a type of proposition in Dewey's logic, is an assertion attributing a mode-of-being or mode-of-action to a determinate situation.
>
> —Tom Burke[14]

So what are judgments? What register do they operate on? How should we understand them? How should they be deployed?

The first point to underscore is that judgments operate on a logical register different from either affirmation (propositions) or truth (metaphysics); rather they function as *warrantably assertible* or not:

> As for what warrants a judgment, a theory of inquiry will have to include a number of criteria for gauging the success of inquiries. Such criteria would include various epistemological and methodological considerations such as whether or not the subject matter of inquiry is being articulated in a coherent way, whether or not the expected results of ongoing activities are satisfied, whether or not such coherence and empirical adequacy are stable, whether or

not there are better ways to proceed, whether or not the results are useful or otherwise applicable to other inquiries, and so forth.[15]

Judgments concern not only veridictional aspects of a situation but following our elaboration of this logic, subjectivational and jurisdictional ones as well.

Such a warrant is not meant as timeless and universal, although it does have a certain degree of generality and a scope of applicability which must be specified as suits the type or kind of case under examination:

> Such evaluations of current experience can be warranted but where the warrantability is limited in scope by the boundedness of that experience.[16]

Judgments are *midstream pragmatic reductions* as a previously discordant and/or indeterminate situation has been brought to a state of *actuality*. They operate on the threshold between the actual and the contemporary.

Vindication

> Ita fac, mi Lucili: vindica te tibi, et tempus quod adhuc aut auferebatur aut subripiebatur aut excidebat collige et serva.
>
> Do this, my Lucilius. Reclaim possession of yourself, for yourself, and whatever time was up till now taken away, was siphoned off, or fell away—gather it up and save it.
>
> —Seneca, Letter #1 to Lucilius[17]

In 1983, before launching into several months of blistering, path-opening textual explication around the themes of frank speech as a veridictional mode and the governance of the self and others in antiquity, Foucault began with two hours dedicated to the minor text by Kant, "What Is Enlightenment?" The connection, to summarize briefly, is the problem of where truth speaking, pedagogy, and critical reflection ought to be directed and how to do so?

We have repeatedly found the questions from "What Is Enlightenment?" to be central to our project. Although the precision with which we were able to pose these questions has altered, become more refined, and so on, the general orientation has been consistent for some time. One of the clarifications we made by writing *Demands* was that an important aspect of producing an *object* of knowledge out of participant-observational inquiry involved changing one's position and one's attitude toward that object. Perhaps this is one of the things John Dewey was pointing at when he wrote,

> The problem reduced to its lowest terms is whether inquiry can develop in its own ongoing course the logical standards and forms to which further inquiry shall submit.[18]

In our ongoing course we have produced objects of knowledge that we qualify as *actual*. In our previous work, the demand was to produce a configuration that captured the discordant qualities which we had found to be component elements of the situations into which we had been inquiring.

Our next challenge, we now understood, was to work on the appropriate standards and forms for transforming the problem of *bios* from its location in configurations of the actual into a constituent object in the process of form-giving within an anthropology of the contemporary.[19]

On returning to Foucault and his reading of the Roman Stoics, particularly Seneca (4 BC–65 AD), it seemed clear that the combination of changing position, posture, and attitude toward an object of attention or thought, in time, was a critical practice of transformation of a relation to that object and to the time of that exercise. Foucault himself returned to the Stoics, and Seneca in particular, because it was in the thought of Seneca that Foucault identified an "event," which he judged to be "still significant for our modern mode of being subjects."[20] While working through Seneca's *Moral Letters* and his works in other genres, it appeared that the event of which Foucault spoke in his lecture was the manner in which Seneca had squarely faced the question of how a form of thinking and writing has temporal and ethical effects on that which one seeks or claims to know.

Classicist James Ker writes of Seneca's description of his epistolary practice "that his letters will help their addressee in an act of *vindicare* performed on the self (*te*), and more specifically on time (*tempus*)."[21] His first letter, on caring for one's time, introduces a distinct inflection of the term *vindicare*, which was technically a Roman juridical term. The connotations of juridical justification, in Seneca's use, are transformed into a theme of the restive relation to the possession and detachment of experience for those seeking to know and care for themselves. As Ker writes, for Seneca, the challenge for thought and writing was the work of possession and a degree of liberty in one's use of time; such work is between writer and reader and has a formative aim.

As Ker judges the issue, what is distinctive about Seneca is that he criticizes Cicero (106–43 BC) and Augustus (63–14 BC) for failing to provide an adequate *vindicatio* of time in the life of the author or reader. Seneca's predecessors' writings fail to do this on account of their incapacity to "render things present" (*prae*). Rather than focus on the present, an important Stoic theme, Seneca writes that Cicero and Augustus, like so many others, are occupied and fixated with hopes and fears for the future. For this reason they flee the present and neglect the task of rendering their experience of the present, rather than, as we would understand it, working through (*durcharbeiten*) the present.

Stoic philosophers privileged the fact that the present is the one part of time we can take possession of and use. For Seneca this fact indexes a fundamental distinction between the time of a moral life and the time in which a person lives. The latter is a time of flux in representations, hopes for the future, and regrets about past actions. The work of the present for Seneca, rather, should be the work of appropriating and vindicating these objects of thought. As a step toward achieving this goal Seneca urges Lucilius to pay attention to the form or forms required to achieve this goal: daily practice of writing. Such a practice entails discipline, attention to *logos*, and the transformation of *logos* into *paraskeuē*, an ethical shorthand of the more general *logos*. The epistolary genre for this practice of transformation can "render present" the necessary virtues by producing an appropriate ratio of the present and nonpresent. In sum, the epistolary form is an essential piece of equipment in a *bios* worth living.

The letter as ethical form transforms the experience of time of the world into a moral, edificatory time in which author and reader can attend to the object clarified through the form of what is being written, with the ultimate aim that reader and writer may freely possess both time and themselves. Curiously, "possession by rendering present" produces a "distanciation" from past and future presents. That is, external presents are cultivated as an intersubjective, textual "rendered present," or what one might think of as a self-sufficient present.

A central and unsurpassable blockage point in taking Stoic philosophy as a resource for an anthropological practice capable of making judgments (the attribution of a mode of being or action to a situation), however, is the Stoic emphasis on *ataraxia*. *Ataraxia* is the absence of inner turmoil and the capacity of a subject to control their thoughts, actions, and passions, such that the subject is undisturbed by unexpected, fortunate or unfortunate events. This state is pursued by the radical affective separation of the time of the everyday and the time of moral edification.

Foucault's careful reappropriation of Seneca and his comparison with Marcus Aurelius provides a major resource for thinking about these limitations. He points out very clearly the theme of motion toward and motion away from the world as part of the exercise of caring for oneself and others. Writing of Seneca's separation between two times, Foucault points out a crucial aspect:

> What seems to me essential, or anyway typical in Hellenistic and Roman conversion, is that if there is a break, it is not produced within the self. There is not that caesura within the self by which the self tears itself away from itself and renounces itself in order to be reborn other than itself after a figurative death. If there is a break—and there is—it takes place with regard to what surrounds the self. The break must be carried out with what surrounds the self so that it is no longer enslaved, dependent, and constrained.[22]

Our theme of *vindicare* is clarified here with respect to the question of the Stoic's relation to the world. One might have thought that the aim of Stoic philosophy is to secede from one's engagements, and that such a retreat is necessary to possess one's own time, as a condition of claiming possession over oneself.

Looking at several passages from Foucault's engagement with Seneca helps dispel this reading. Foucault asks, from what does the gaze turn away when it turns toward the self? First of all, one turns away from others, and second of all things of the world. He points out an important paradox, one whose implications we will need to unpack and think through for anthropology:

> The way in which this turning away of the gaze from others to oneself must be carried out does not consist at all in substituting oneself for the other as the object of a possible or necessary knowledge.[23]

Rather, it involves a "movement" or "shift." Such a movement or shift for Seneca, or the Stoics, is toward "the secrets of nature." The paradox is then crystalized:

> How is it at this point that Seneca couples with this objective [of turning away from others and things of the world] . . . the possibility and necessity of *exploring* the world?[24]

Turning the gaze toward the self, and away from "things of the world," requires the exploration of the secrets of nature. Why a return to nature? Seneca's answer: Because then one is free by the law of nature and not by the law of the city. Free for what? To overcome servitude to the self. This is then the paradoxical sequence: return to the self is a break with the environment, which involves a turn toward nature, so as one can escape servitude to the obligations of the civic self.

Motion

"A return to nature" is a turn to motion; after having located what moves—the subject—Foucault asks the modal question: How is it that this subject moves? What kind of motion? Seneca addressed his dialogue *On the Tranquility of Mind* to a young prefect in Nero's guard called Serenus. In the text, the young guard is given the role of asking for a cure for his mental disturbances; he tells Seneca that he practices Stoic philosophy, readily following Zeno, Cleanthes, and Chrysippus, successive heads of the Stoa. There are, however, moments when he is dazzled by luxury; "none of these things alters me," Seneca has him recount, "but none fails to unsettle me."[25] He describes this unsettling with an analogy to a natural phenomenon: "It is not a storm I labor under, but a sea-sickness." The analogy is significant; the issue is not an external "event" affecting the subject, displacing him as he pursues his course. Rather, the problem is the motion itself. Seneca characterizes the problem in the following way:

> Everyone is in the same predicament, both those who are tormented by inconstancy and boredom and an unending change of purpose . . . and those who idle away their time, yawning. Add to them those that twist and turn like insomniacs, trying all manner of positions until in their weariness they find repose."[26]

Seneca compares the malady of the insomniac changing position to the people who undertake far-ranging travel, changing scene and view constantly: "One journey after another they embark on, one spectacle they exchange for another. As Lucretius says, 'thus each man ever flees himself.'"[27]

If in his dialogue with Serenus the problem of motion is clarified, its remediation is considered elsewhere. With respect to the pathos of motion, of pursuing the practice in which one is engaged, Seneca prescribes a curative movement—a "stepping back" from the point we occupy in space: "Transitory events will take on their real proportions again when through this stepping back we reach the highest point where the secrets of the whole world will be open to us."[28]

Of course, this stepping back to the "summit" from which all will be revealed is predicated on participation with the Stoic conception of the divine
reason and of nature. Such participation aids a subject to put the world into
view; what we thought were great events, or transformations, were mere
points in space governed by laws of nature. Hence the aim of the return
is not to remove the subject from the world, but to make a real judgment
about the subject and the world, in relation to the standards and forms of
nature.

Our aim is not to jettison anthropology in favor of Stoic philosophy,
no more than Foucault thought that Stoic philosophy was an answer to the
troubles of philosophical and political thinking today. Clearly, whatever
form we seek to make, the Stoic cosmology of nature and divine reason
linking *anthrōpos* and nature is not an option.

THREE

Forms

It is easy to believe that a culture is more attached to its values than its forms; that the latter can be easily modified, abandoned, taken up once again, because only meaning (sens) is deeply rooted. To do so is to misunderstand how forms, when they come undone or are born can provoke astonishment or arouse hatred; it is to misunderstand that people are more attached to the manner of seeing, of saying, of doing and of thinking than that which they see, think, say or do. The battle of forms in the West has been as ferocious, if not more, than that of ideas and values.

—Michel Foucault[1]

Today, we observe that deeply etched but largely unmapped fault lines between values, ideas, and forms reverberate beneath the topology of the present. The fact that values are to be found everywhere should not be surprising in a world dominated and saturated by consumer capitalism and global finance. After all, citizens are obliged, polled, and mandated to have values, to uphold values; and they are persistently encouraged to create, maintain, and express value in their lives.

The professorate is hardly exempt from the value mandate and many have eagerly contributed to its spread and its legitimacy. In that eagerness, however, there is a price to be paid as values and ideas are frequently conflated. As anthropologists, we note that the incessant proliferation and association of ideas and values is a mandatory aspect of contemporary life. Even when ideas and values are distinguished, one of the primary demands on the smaller group of professors who still see their work as exploring ideas is to make explicit and to highlight connections between ideas and values.

Making these connections communicable, or so it is constantly claimed and demanded, will establish the value of ideas in the real world, or so the philanthropic foundations, technology transfer offices, earnest graduate students, and so on, hector us (and themselves).

Decades ago, Gilles Deleuze mocked (and warned us against) this obligation to communicate, to be of the moment, to get your ideas across in an accessible manner. The question remains: Accessible to whom? And in what form? In 1994, Deleuze wrote:

> Finally the most shameful moment came when computer science, marketing, design, and advertising, all the disciplines of communication, seized hold of the word *concept* itself and said: "This is our concern, we are the creative ones, we are the *ideas men*! We are the friends of the concept; we put it in our computers." Information and creativity, concept and enterprise; there is already an abundant bibliography.
>
> Marketing has preserved the idea of a certain relationship between the concept and the event. But here the concept has become the set of product displays (historical, scientific, artistic, sexual, pragmatic), and the event has become the exhibition that sets up various displays and the "exchange of ideas" it is supposed to promote. The only events are exhibitions, and the only concepts are products that can be sold.[2]

Lest we forget, Deleuze was warning of the ascendency of the ideas men and women at a time when even in his darkest hour, he could not dream of Twitter and Facebook: "No thinking, please, we are communicating with our thousands of friends with pictures and 128 characters."

Philosophy arose, Deleuze explains, when a form was invented in which friends engaged in concept work—agonistically.[3] Philosophy arose in a specific venue—the agora—where "a community of free men as rivals" engaged each other in contests of the utmost seriousness. They were friends and citizens. That world is long since gone. Today, for Deleuze the challenge of philosophy consists of a "modest pedagogy of the concept, which would have to analyze the conditions of creation as factors" in thinking and form-giving.[4]

Anthropological inquiry, we add, is both propaedeutic to and fundamentally necessary for adequately undertaking the identification and re-fashioning of those factors. Inventing venues in which such repurposing can take place, as well as the forms in which concepts would contribute to the growth of capacities without intensifying nefarious power relations, stands forth as a primary demand of the day.

Forms and Formalism

Forms—their existence, creation, maintenance, and destruction—constitute a problem. What, for example, the anthropologist wonders, are the contemporary practices through which relations of values, ideas, and forms are established, transmitted, authorized, and imposed or excluded? How might one conduct an inquiry into that topic? How, furthermore, could one find the right way to conduct such an inquiry? The problem, fortunately, has from time to time received some attention.

In 1982, when Foucault published his homage to his friend, the composer, conductor, and musician Pierre Boulez (from which the opening quote is taken), echoes of past reception battles Foucault had been subjected to and had participated in, lingered; their incisions were scarred in his memory, lingered. Foucault retained acrid memories of his own intrepid attempts to experiment with formalizing systems of discourse, the best form to give them, and his attempts to justify those experiments reflectively in terms both conceptually and polemically.

In retrospect, once, with the course of time and the erasures wrought by the fickleness of fashions in Parisian intellectual life, it became clearer that the decisive stakes of these spiteful exchanges turned not on who was correct or incorrect intellectually but rather ultimately on the right of a thinker, of a researcher, of a writer, to undertake experiments in form per se—whether they succeeded or not, whatever might be meant at the time by success.[5]

With a decade and a half's distance from the mid-60s skirmishes over the status of textuality, Foucault was in a position to reflect on (albeit not exactly with either dispassion or irony) the derogatory reactions to his attempts at epistemic form-giving in *The Order of Things*, and its rigorous apology in the ancient sense of the term, *The Archaeology of Knowledge*. Earlier, the conceptually systematic approach and dexterous literary manner of presentation of these works had been dismissively framed by both left- and right-wing critics as denigrating the value and meaning of the human.

The justification of the ferocity of the vilification turned on Foucault's attempt at displacement of the subject's centrality in the production, circulation, and ultimately the worth of ideas and values. Said another way, Foucault's experiments with conceptual and discursive form-giving had been both the site, and the cause, of the polemic reaction. Years later, it is hard to fathom the depth of feeling, but to fail to do so would be

> to fail to understand that the manner of seeing, saying, making and thinking
> is held to be more important than what one sees, thinks and does.[6]

In retrospect the critics' intensity can justifiably be seen as exotic but also symptomatic of the vital importance of manners of seeing, doing, thinking even more, as Foucault observed, than what is done, thought, said, and seen.

Rather than continuing to answer attacks as he had done previously for a short period of time, or to ignore his critics, eventually Foucault had learned to turn certain topics that had occasioned polemics into sites of problematization. In his homage to Boulez, he gives us an example of how one might address the symptomatic conceptually; he mused on the conjuncture of affect, indicative diagnostically of a historical moment of problematization when settled things began to be unsettled and unsettling. "Things," he wrote,

> have taken a singular allure; it is the "formal" itself, it is the reflective work on systems of forms that has become the stakes of moral, aesthetic and political confrontations marked by a remarkable hostility.[7]

One might have introduced the then recent battles over positivism in the social and cultural sciences or the emergence of pop art with its contemptuous overturning of the formal primacy of modern art, or the Beatles.[8]

Present and Actual Foyers

Collaboration, we have determined, has proved extremely valuable to us for inventing and experimenting with a logic of thinking that can aid thinkers to move from the present toward the contemporary. If we had not reactivated the venue, we may have taken up the same topics, in a cooperative fashion, mediated by distance and time. Without a venue, and without having worked through the motion from the present to the actual, together, it could not provide a *foyer d'expérience*. This means that the activation of a series of venues is necessary to facilitate bringing together forms of possible knowledge, normative matrices of conduct and virtual modes of existence for possible subjects. Furthermore, without having passed through a certain amount of collaborative work, asking how we were problematizing these objects, we would not be able to take up prior *foyers d'expérience* as objects of reflection, and hence would not be able to participate in or observe the contemporary.

2007: *Foyer d'expérience* Set in the Present

We gradually came to understand that the various phases of experience and experiment, over the course of six years, had different but mutually dependent logics, providing different standards and forms, appropriate to each phase. In 2007, given developments in the biosciences, to the question of what was being problematized, the answer, Rabinow and Bennett proposed, was the *figure* of *anthrōpos*.[9] To the question of what is emergent, they had hypothesized that the answer was the *figure* of *synthetic anthrōpos*. We regulated our inquiry on the basis of this hypothesis.[10]

The experiment with the biosciences was conducted on the basis of prior experiences. We had accepted to engage in a series of projects designed to interface the human sciences, biosciences, and ethics, because these projects seemed to provide the conditions for timely experiments and experiences. One might say that these conditions seemed to have had the potential to be or to form a *foyer d'expérience*, a crucible of experience, in which veridictional, subjectivational, and jurisdictional aspects were mutually at play.

The problem space had seemed to be one in which it was clear that in our diverse inquiries, we should refuse older reoccupations and that we should search to occupy a different problem space, which we held to be at least possibly emergent at that time. We refused the reoccupation of culture and nature. Although *anthrōpos* was a general candidate for the problem space we wanted to occupy, we were reminded not to give in to our impatience.

We rejected an ironic stance toward developments in the manner of science studies; rather, from the start this experiment was one of participant-observation and hence of experiment and experience. After initial participant-observation it was clear that whatever was going on contained some fundamental discordancies and indeterminacies. This set of experiences had motivated us to retreat to a venue where we could attempt to diagnose the logic of the situation in broad terms. It would be fair to say that what we called later a *venue haven* was itself a *foyer d'expérience*, albeit not the one that we had set out to work on.

This moment or stage differed from the history of the present in that making the present contingent was hardly necessary. Rather, we began to conceptualize the fact that we didn't know logically what kind of object the present was. Once we began that reflection we were eventually led to take up the present logically as part of a series: present, actual, contemporary. Since we knew that we hoped to get to the contemporary, this was one of many lessons in patience which taught us that the required logical steps remained to be invented, experienced, experimented with, and conceptualized. At that point we came to realize later that we were immersed in the present; however, we engaged in intense diagnostic work which provided initial distance and equipment in order to continue the inquiry.

The diagnostic orientation had been to ask: Is something being refigured in the problem space of the biosciences, human sciences, and ethics? We were equipped diagnostically to step back into the present to continue inquiry. Discordancies and indeterminacies in participant-observation could be identified with the help of the diagnostic as sites of further inquiry, rather than only as *stultitia* producing experiences. It enabled us to go back to the inquiry as itself a crucible of experience, one in which veridictional, ethical, and subjectivational relations were at stake and about which we were on the road to establishing determinations and propositions.

The determinations and propositions were of the order that Geertz named (i.e., that there are problems which can be diagnosed), about which one can do little to *reconstruct*. As this situation became clear and progressed, conceptualizing the discordancies came to the fore as the task of inquiry.

At a certain point, the results of this stage of the experiment were ones we could establish as determinations. We tested them repeatedly and eventually decided that continued repetition could not teach us anything new and was hardly enjoyable. Hence for scientific and ethical reasons it was time to complete that stage of participant-observation.[11]

Our experiences of stasis were catalyzed such that we could and knew we should leave the field. This was a decision, as the possibility of remaining affiliated with these organizations was offered to us. Despite the money, it was clear that they were no longer the kind of *foyers d'expérience* that we had set out in the first place to engage with. We determined that the limits of the present were modern ones and that in the present there was little hope for a contemporary remediation of the relation of ethics and bioscience.[12] Since we sought to experiment and experience the contemporary, we had to leave the field.

2011: *Foyer d'expérience* Set in the Actual

Once this decision had been taken, we could begin to conceptualize our experience, so as to provide appropriate distance and motion. This work consisted in inventing equipment, the studio, so that our practice could change given that the objects on which we were focused and the objectives we were seeking to obtain were different from those of the previous *foyer*. We recognized that for this venue to operate under these new conditions it should be more of an atelier than a haven.

With this studio equipment we turned to logic work by undertaking a conceptualization of our prior experience and experiment. As this work proceeded it became clear that we were no longer operating amid the daily banalities and irritations of the present. As we freed ourselves from double binds and *stultitia* we realized we were working in a space of the actual. We determined that this was a necessary space of affective and conceptual work- ing over and through the experiences of the discordancies and limits of the present as objects. In its own right this logical clarification, we saw, began to constitute a *foyer d'expérience*.

Demands worked through the logic of our practice, showing how we con- tinued to examine the conduct of our inquiry, the ethical relation to our- selves, those with whom we had worked, the technically mediated objects of *bios*, and the discordances with which we were grappling. There were two aspects to this working through (*durcharbeiten*); one was to ask ourselves what the next step could be beyond "problem identification" in attempted colabor, in the present. How, in other words, to pose further more precise questions about the significance of the problem identified? How to carry on doing anthropological inquiry, after fieldwork: reworking, rethinking, and curating the knowledge gained in fieldwork, but in such a way that did not understand the full process of inquiry as consisting in a set of repre- sentations of those experiences. Rather, much conceptual and experimental work, we argued, was required subsequently. The diagnosis for this further work was to be found in Michel Foucault's identification of the separation of knowledge and care by method.[13]

Our original objective in attempting collaboration was to think about the scientific form of life (anthropological and biological) which could bring together reflection on the biological objects being produced and the ramifi- cations of such inventions. *Demands* was a phenomenology of sort tracking the movement out of the field (the present) so as to objectify the discord- ances of collaboration (the actual configuration of discordancy). We began to address the question of what stance we could take toward these con- figurations of discordancy. This question of stance was aided by transform- ing the problem of collaboration, in its present and actual modalities—as problematic experience and diagnostic marker—into a problematization of *bios*. With this shift, we were in a position to take up, in a renewed man- ner, three core aspects that we had identified as part of configurations of discordancy in the actual: justification and truth telling (how a subject puts himself on the side of the good and the right); the metrics through which collaboration could be judged; and the figures of *anthrōpos* being actualized in the sciences today.

The experience itself opened up a different form of participant- observation and collaboration. We considered this anthropological once we became clear about what kind of a practice this was. This clarity was provided in part by the logical work we were undertaking.[14]

With the thematization of the problematization of *bios* and of the problem of *technē tou biou*, we were in a position to pose questions in a second-order manner about truth telling, metrics, and figures: whether in the midst of discordance, excess and deficiency, there might be a series of means we could identify. We came to see that we needed a more precise analytic to identify appropriate ethical questions. Thus, a further logical step was to ask what further transformations were required to move from the actual toward the contemporary. Eventually we decided that we needed to be clearer about what Foucault has called the ethical fourfold, an analytic device for ethical inquiry, so that we could identify on what, how, and toward what end we required conceptual clarity and equipmental invention.

Ethical Fourfold

To the aids [parastēmata] which have been mentioned let this one still be added: Make for yourself a definition or description of the thing which is presented to you, so as to see what kind of a thing it is in its substance, in its nudity, in its complete entirety, and tell yourself its proper name, and the names of the things of which it has been compounded, and into which it will be resolved.

—Marcus Aurelius[15]

Like the term *problematization*, Michel Foucault wrote relatively little about what he called the *ethical fourfold*.[16] The terms in the series were designed for a specific historical inquiry and meant to serve a specific purpose—differentiating the Ancient Greek concerns over sexuality from those of the early Christians. Foucault spent a great deal of time, only minimal traces of which are available in his published writing, making clear how challenging it was to use a term like *sexuality* and then to demonstrate how the term had been composed of historically different concepts and referents as responses or solutions to a general if historically locatable ethical challenge or dilemma or paradox or contradiction—or simply discordancy.

The fourfold comprised a series of categories to aid ethical analysis of the free relation to oneself: the *ethical substance*—that which constitutes the object of reflection and practice; the *mode of subjectivation*—how subjects become subjects of an ethically qualified sort, recognizing that they have obligations and that they are capable of practicing them; the telos or ends of that practice—ends which may well be internal or external to that practice; as well as *askēsis*—the ethical exercise to work on the specified substance, toward an end, and to become that subject of an ethically qualified kind.[17]

Foucault made clear in his published interviews that he believed that the ethical fourfold and the type of problems it had arisen to address had a potentially wide-ranging generality, possibly applicable as a heuristic over large swaths of time as well as a range of diverse problems. The term's continuity lay in its capacity to provide the distinctions that could be used to highlight the conceptual and equipmental contours of ethical reflection and practice.

We are experimenting with using the ethical fourfold as equipment both to guide us in inventing forms, concepts, and equipment, as well as to illuminate to whatever degree possible, the pathways and transformations required in order to move from the *actual* to the *contemporary*.

We decided we needed to reflect more on why our use of the fourfold seemed helpful at this juncture—why there is a shift of scale (diminishing) and possibly of generality. Since we hoped to move further—and knew we should (*sollen*)—and since it seemed like we could (*können*), the fourfold provided a form and a standard which could reorient us from past determinations toward sites for future observation.

The two terms and the two parts of the fourfold which provided major signposts for the pathway and transformations to a form and equipment toward which we were stumbling were *parastēma* and *vindicare*. Upon reflection, they were terms that opened an active and affirmative set of options, in order to create the motion toward the contemporary. Thus, to arrive successfully at a state of vindication meant that the constantly reactive, stultifying, and ultimately withering position one had been cornered in—not only by the bioscientists but increasingly by other social scientists and to a degree by ourselves—could be countered actively and positively in a Nietzschean sense.

In situations of double binds, especially those in which one had to a certain degree entered voluntarily, there seemed to be an obligation to take account as well as to give an account of why and how it was obligatory to change one's subject position. Only by so doing could the growth of capacities stand a chance of being disentangled from the intensification of power relations.

That is to say, given a state of abiding unequal power relations that were being alternately exercised as negligence, exclusion, or domination, if one wanted to counter (agonistically or otherwise) the continuing ethical and veridictional denigration, then vindication appeared to be the required mode of subjectivation. One was not alone: there was a lineage of *vindicare* with its equipment, its forms, its *können und sollen*.

The identification of the concept and practice of vindication was a major step beyond the options proposed by Albert Hirschman; exit, voice, loyalty. It also constituted a more productive gambit under these condi-tions than secession. Secession, a lateral move out of a situation of paradox or dilemma which one could evade or elude through a frame shift was ena-bling but not vindicatory.

For these motions to take place, however, there would have had to be a prior foundational discovery and affirmation, again in the Nietzschean sense. That prior affirmation turned on the term *parastēma*. Unless one could affirm the possibility of an ethical substance, a core capacity, in which a mode of truth and a mode of conduct could have an integral and integrat-ing relationship, it would seem extremely unlikely that the rest of the four-fold could be made to operate in the manner we were seeking. One could justify, for example, or perhaps even vindicate the ethics of one's endeavor or its warranted assertibility but bringing them into a mutually formative dynamic seemed like a distant horizon both in our own experiences as well as in the history of philosophy which has interminably sought foundations (ontological, epistemological, quasi-transcendental, etc.) in order to make them cohere.

We did not wish *parastēma* into existence; rather we suffered from its absence, its neglect; we suffered from those nihilists who in one manner or another asserted and commanded its negation. These remarks refer back to our inquiry in which we demonstrated that within the actual configurations of discordancy there could be no bringing together of a practice of truth and conduct (understood broadly). Moving from the actual configurations of discordancy in which we had been participant observers, schismogenic ragamuffins of the double binds, to the configuration of the actual, it gradu-ally became clear that motion and form-giving were desirable and desired, possibly even at hand. It was only with that discovery and its reappropria-tion that we could counter, not merely escape from the stasis of the active nihilism that ruled the day.

We needed to be vigilant. To simply proclaim a mode of subjectivation, or for that matter its impossibility, was the kind of purely discursive move we had long since been alert to avoid. Hence it was only after the long practice of inquiry and its curation and then the acknowledgment that one aspect or facet of a current problematization had to be identified if a "pos-sible solution" existed that we could proceed. We needed to have some self-assurance that the problem space we were about to enter was worth oc-cupying. It was not, as Blumenberg had alerted us, a problem space which we as modern had no right either to despise or to make our own.

In order to decide whether we were about to occupy a problem space that could be made contemporary, we needed to know and feel that the very best of our predecessors had found themselves landlocked as it were. Blumenberg and Geertz provided the essential GPS of modernity as concerns nature and culture. The challenge consequently was to shift the exploration to the terrain of *bios*, to clarify our *können und sollen*, to inspect our existing equipment, and to set out patiently to give form where it was missing: that space where only values and ideas abounded. If we could take up this task and this obligation in an appropriate manner we would have achieved, at the very least, another *Ausgang*, this time from the *actual* and its configurations.

Fourfold: Standards and Forms

We decided we needed to pose the question: In what did vindication consist as part of the motion out of the actual? Consequently we proceeded to reactivate our venue and began to assemble terms. We saw no reason not to reaffirm *eudaemonia* as our telos. The fourfold was a plausible candidate to aid us in articulating a form in which we might come to understand the interconnections of the subjectivational and veridictional stakes of the motion we knew needed to be explored. Taken up as equipment, the fourfold aided in designating the object of work in this motion: the problematic distance between truth and conduct as an object of reflection. The challenge was to produce a *technē tou biou* appropriate to the situation. This situation consists in the search for the remediation of older *technē tou biou* which were appropriate to inquiry, and the problem spaces in which they were invented and practiced. By so doing we anticipated opening up a range of motion.

> Ethical substance: *Parastēma*
> Askesis: *Technē tou biou*
> Mode of Subjectivation: *Vindicare*
> Telos: *Eudaemonia*

Flourishing: *Eudaemonia*

At this juncture we understood that we had to do the work of transforming calls for self-justification into possessing freely the warranted claims that we could make about the actual and its demands. We had shown that self-justification was a deficiency and that the excess would be to ignore or be satisfied with the work we had done, as having already answered this challenge of truth and conduct.

The identification of the need for a mean could be imagined to be what the *daemon* was whispering in our ears. Following Aristotle, it is crucial to remember that the mean is never an essence. The mean is demarcated by what has been called an *horos*, a boundary or measure. Hence, the problem of *eudaemonia* for us at this juncture was to find a mean.

In book 6 of the *Ethics*, Aristotle writes that one of the objects of ethics is choices in and ways of doing an activity. The mode in which reflection on such objects occurs, he claims, should be through virtue oriented to correct reasoning. Correct reason is characterized by the aims or targets of the one who possesses such reason. Crucially, Aristotle uses the term *horos*, which is more acutely translated, as Harris Rackman does, by the term *standard*:

There is a certain *standard* determining these *modes* of observing the mean.[18]

Fundamentally, it is not enough to *know* what having the state of the mean is, to know about virtue. Rather it is necessary to know by what standard the mean is brought about.[19] The fact that Aristotle never actually names this standard substantively has left Western philosophy with the long durational problems of the relations among and between *logoi*, *bios*, and *eudaemonia*.

Fourfold: The Actual

Given the problematization that we have diagnosed, and given our inquiries that provided the subjectivational and veridictional experiences and insights that warranted our diagnosis, we need to make explicit how each term functions with respect to this problem space, so that it can be subjected to scrutiny.

The production of a tentative ethical fourfold, taken up as equipment, aided us in giving form to our motion from the actual configurations toward another ontological state. A candidate to meet this challenge would have to activate a mean between an excess and deficiency, of relating truth and conduct. The fourfold facilitated the process of identification and specified that at least one determination of this mean, for our work, would have to traverse the recent past, the actual and the near future.

A central task was to think about and identify that state; the first candidate was the virtual. The virtual was a promising candidate because etymologically it indexes virtue, understood as "excellence, potency, and efficacy." The term could be understood as capacity. In that light, after having configured the actual, the question was how do we activate capacities for further motion?

Ethical Substance

Our genealogical labor has shown us a discordancy in modernity, the sundering of truth and conduct. Both Weber and Geertz separated truth and conduct in the name of disinterestedness that too quickly eliminated the ethical as connected to the warrantable. This separation led to two dead ends: Weber's misdiagnosis of the truth side, science, led to an exaggerated formulation of the autonomy of the conduct side. Geertz's impoverished view of the conduct side, led to a stunted understanding of the truth side. Both Weber and Geertz captured the actual configurations of discordancy, but did not reproblematize whether you could move to configure the actual. By configuring the actual, the possibility of motion beyond it is opened up.

Askēsis: Technē tou biou

Foucault showed us that Seneca, among many others, had devoted a great deal of care and thought to the practices of *technē tou biou*. Obviously, once again, we cannot simply reappropriate past solutions. Rather, past problems and solutions need to be repurposed and refactored. This refactoring turns on bringing the repurposed *logoi* to bear on a newly introduced ethical substance.

Even the effort to experiment with a repurposing has provoked demands for self-justification. *Vindicare* for Seneca and Lucilius was oriented to *ataraxia* in and from the present. The counterpoint to *ataraxia*, we claim, is restiveness. This restiveness doubly provokes calls for self-justification; not only on the *logos* side but also on the conduct side, demands which in our experience can never be satisfied. The call can never be satisfied, not because we had nothing to say, but because given their modes of subjectivation, others were incapable of listening. Let us remember that Seneca picks out listening as the starting point for thinking and philosophy. Plutarch picks it out as the starting point to exit immaturity. Given that self-justification was a dead end, we needed a substitute.

Mode of Subjectivation: *Vindicare*

Once we understood we needed a substitute for self-justification as the only way to move from actual configurations to a configuration of the actual, a configuration we could work both in and on, Seneca's concept of *vindicare* (possession of oneself, one's time and the actuality of the situation one finds oneself in) seemed like the right concept. Furthermore, it seemed that it could be used to produce the right manner of bringing truth and conduct together.

For Seneca and Lucilius the form was the exchange of letters. For us, in order to make *parastēma* part of a practice, one needed to possess and make actual the veridictional side as well as the conduct side. *Vindicare* was a cover term to at least indicate what this practice could be. It was not self-justification in that it had eliminated a communicational and defensive response, through its production via inquiry of a significant body of work and the growing understanding that this work could only have been performed if there was from the start a *technē tou biou* with a metric beyond instrumentality. For us the appropriate form for *vindicare* is repurposed with respect to collaborative inquiry. *Vindicare* is not individual; the form presupposes and contributes to a practice of *philia* and *sophia*.

Available Forms: From Figures to *Syndialēpsis*

> Evaluations, in essence, are not values but ways of being, modes of existence of those who judge and evaluate, serving as principles for the values on the basis of which they judge. This is why we always have the beliefs, feelings and thoughts that we deserve given our way of being or our style of life.
>
> —Gilles Deleuze[20]

Our curiosity about how to move beyond the actual was directed by the activation of the terms we assembled through the ethical fourfold. Philologist June Allison, in her book on Thucydides, *Power and Preparedness in Thucydides*, reminds us that all equipment (*paraskeuē*) is composed of *logoi*; as such, in the face of proliferating truth claims, and with the challenge of bringing truth and conduct together in the face of such proliferation, what we required was a *pragmatic reduction* of the available *logoi*, taken up as *paraskeuē*, repurposed for the task at hand—to move beyond the actual.[21]

Crucially, since we already had a venue in which to bring together *technē tou biou*, a vindicatory mode of subjectivation and work on the ethical substance of truth and conduct (*parastēma*), we were then in a position to focus on the challenge of specifying the mean. During our work on the actual and its configurations, in the *venue atelier* we had identified and analyzed two key forms: figures and narrative modes. As it turned out these corresponded to two stages of the work as objects to be determined and judged. Forms of figuration were a central anchor point during the elaboration of the diagnostic; narrative form was a core thematic during the inquiry itself as well as during the work on the actual in the *venue atelier*.

Rabinow and Bennett had initially posited in their diagnostic the figure of *synthetic anthrōpos* as a placeholder but concluded during the course of the inquiry that there was no warrant to assert its existence under present conditions, although certain discursive constructions have attempted to write or speak it into existence. While there may well be a future figure of *bios* in which truth and conduct are inseparable, as Foucault shows us had been the case for Aurelius in the Stoic cosmos, only time will tell.

Another alternative is that there might be a future figure of *bios* in which truth and conduct are radically separate. We consider this alternative as a deficit, as it would place ethical conduct in a subsidiary role with no possible way of refiguring *bios logos*. The excess side would be the politically correct versions of science, in which the moral framework is known in advance, applied by a discursive police force, and in which the veridictional questions would be subsidiary to the moral ones.

Narrative Forms: Lēpsis

Our initial efforts to move through the participant-observational stage of the inquiry and then to curate the configurations of the actual turned on the identification and deployment of *metalēpsis* as the appropriate narrative mode in which to operate.[22] *Metalēpsis* is a participatory mode, in which terms or characters participate with one another either in the past or the future. In that mode, at least in the manner in which we were using it, the aim was for reader and writer to be interpolated into the text under construction so as to project a future reconstruction.

During the gathering and curation stage, what we were searching for was a form of "possession," or "seizing," a *lēpsis*. The move from the actual configurations of discordancy to the configurations of the actual demonstrated that we had reached the limits of a *metaleptic* mode. If one is engaged in a project of participant-observation, then narrative form alone, while useful in indicating possible directions of practice, is itself ultimately a piece of equipment that can be blocked by the exercise of unequal power relations. Discursive capacities and capacities that can be practiced are not the same thing.

The actual configurations of *bios*, warranted by inquiry, were composed of both *technē* and *logos*. We established that deficiencies and excesses abounded in the configuration. While their identification is necessary, the ultimate objective at this stage was the completion of the series, the identification and specification of the category of the mean, and the equipment necessary to turn it into a pragmatic reduction.

In order to proceed in filling what we knew to be an essential gap in a series, we thought we must require a form of *lēpsis* but not *metalēpsis*. In order to specify the components of this other as yet unnamed form of *lēpsis*, we determined that on the *technē* side it was mandatory to attend to capacities and to the mode of *pragmatic reduction*. On the *logos* side, it was necessary to attend to forms and practices and to their equipmental functions.

Given that critical limitation, of narrative form, we wondered if nonetheless a different form of *lēpsis*—one that was equipmental and pragmatic— might aid us in leaving the actual. We found a rare, but emboldening term in the *Meditations* of Marcus Aurelius, *syndialēpsis*; *dialēpsis* is best translated as "intellectual work and judgment," and *syndialēpsis*, "intellectual work and judgment undertaken with others." This term seemed to meet the requirements of the pragmatic reduction we were seeking.

Our wager, hence, was that the appropriate *lēpsis* required a "syn" component, which we had established in our work in the *atelier venue*. It also seemed to require a collaborative mode of practice and hence the need for a *syn-dialēpsis*. In Aurelius' use, *syndialēpsis* enables a joint judgment, oriented not at reproach, but at rectification. Aurelius, writing of what he learned from various people, refers to Alexander of Cotiaeum, "the grammarian." What he learned, he tells us, was

> not reproachfully to reprehend any man for a barbarism, or a solecism, or any false pronunciation, but dexterously by way of answer, or testimony, or joint judgment of the same matter (taking no notice of the word) to utter it as it should have been spoken.[23]

What is being rectified? First of all, a clarification of the discursive situation. This work had been substantially done in the articulation of the actual. We now had the liberty to give the mean a prominence which it lacked in the actual. That prominence provided orientation as to a mode of intervention, albeit still discursive.

Given this orientation and given the fourfold, the mode of subjectivation is guided not only by the ethical substance but by this honed rectificatory disposition. Such a disposition is not *ataraxic*, but rather posed as a problem of engaged and critical, if second-order, observation. The path to achieve this dispositional state, it turned out, was through concerted attention to *Gemüt*, self-affectation. For Kant, we will all recall, the *Gemüt* was the ethical substance. For us, searching for a different ethical substance, the *Gemüt* nonetheless proved to be important as the locus of equipmental attention.

The specification and orientation to the actual discursive field and our identification of the need to work on the mean combines with the requirement to build equipment to work over the *Gemüt* so as to open the possibility of a pragmatic reduction of possible ideas, values, and forms to a specified attention on forms.

PART TWO

Toward the Contemporary

INTRODUCTION

That the world, through the *bios*, became that experience through which we know ourselves, that exercise through which we reveal ourselves to ourselves, that exercise through which we transform ourselves or we know ourselves, I think that this is a transformation, an important mutation from the classical Greek thought, in which the *bios* was the object of a *technē*, that is to say a reasonable and rational art.

—Michel Foucault[1]

Part 2 is devoted to exploring the term *contemporary*. To give an epochal definition to the contemporary is more futile and misleading than providing an epochal definition of the modern. Although the contemporary is not a defined historical period it is not without its historicity. The need for a category like the contemporary, however, is not unmotivated or arbitrary. Thus, it seems clear in 2013 that the labels "postmodern," "globalization," "the neoliberal," are a series of largely discursive cover terms denoting fashion trends in the academy. Obviously, the essential nature of world history or politics did not change three times in a few decades. This banality does not mean that these terms have no meaning, but only that they lose their purchase once they become epochal and/or totalizing. For terms to be worth pursuing, they must be taken seriously as terms: rigorous attempts must be made to specify their concepts and referents, as well as the alterations, recombinations, and mutual productivity of such concepts and referents.

In that light, we have attempted to be vigilant and restive in our manner of proceeding with the term *contemporary*. Initially at least, it has been easier to mark moves to be avoided than to delimit the term. A helpful starting point has been to accept provisionally Michel Foucault's claim that modernity is best taken up as an ethos rather than an epoch.[2] We have concluded however, that it must be specified that aspects of an ethos are identifiable on both the subject and object planes: an ethos is both a way of seeing things and, for some duration and for some practices, it is also a quality of worldly relations that is not constructed or interpreted by the observer but has the potential to call forth an interpretation. At a minimum, at the broadest level, an ethos is a stylization of subjectivity and objectivity taken up in its historicity.

Once terms are given modal specification, and once the range of narrative moods available are specified and tested, then whatever generality is achieved can be honed, made available and operative for inquiry and contemporary narration. One way of proceeding toward such terminological clarification is to identify instances of others whose work and lives prove an opportunity to explore and enrich our understanding of the term *contemporary*.

Indeterminacy as a Contemporary Domain

Having carefully considered the results of the logic of our experiments with *bios*, we concluded that it had been only in the restrained crucible of our *atelier-fabrique* that we were able to bring *technē tou biou* into existence. Having posited that the telos of our anthropological vocation on the ethical side was flourishing, we established to our satisfaction that flourishing was not only a term with a long lineage behind it but that it could be actualized today as a practice and an experience. Subsequently, we developed and checked capacities and rectified venues in order to facilitate performing requisite pragmatic reductions. Among these was the articulation of the ethical fourfold. Equipped with the form as well as the constituent terms of our fourfold, we were able to distance ourselves from the experiments we had conducted as participant-observers. In sum, we were in a position to conclude that the phase of the experiment with *bios* had been brought to fruition.

We eventually decided that the next stage of the project had to concern itself with possible forms of *anthrōpos* today. Furthermore, we believed that the status and forms of *anthrōpos* that provided the most salient challenge was to be in a contemporary mode. This hypothesis does not mean that we were abandoning *bios*, but rather, in the dedialecticized, nontranscendental dialectical manner we had made our own, the challenge was to bring forward an ethical substance, mode of subjectivation, *askēsis* and telos to the next stage of the project, now as equipment.

We concluded after a good deal of wondering and wandering, perhaps paradoxically, that the domain that needed to be explored, and for which equipment would need to be invented, was the domain of *indeterminacy* and not *discordancy*. At first blush, this intuition was paradoxical because we had spent so much time designing, conducting, and evaluating inquiry as logic and experience that turned on ethical problems and challenges. We realized, however, that this insight was not paradoxical precisely in that the point of our inquiry had ultimately been an experiment in ethics; consequently it followed that the design of the original project turned on discordancy.

Indeterminacy, for Dewey, turned on thinking, clarification and testing of concepts, pragmatic reductions, and reformulations of situations. Hence the next challenge was to design a topological problem space around an object, *anthrōpos*, which was not uniquely conceptual, but nonetheless which, in certain key dimensions, concerned *logoi*. Again, seemingly paradoxically, we had concluded that the way to approach and take up the contemporary, as both object and style, was not directly through more inquiry; although unless there had been prior inquiry which had provided warrant for configurations of the actual, no further motion would be legitimate. In order to proceed with more clarity in our designs on the contemporary, we need to address the problem of how to characterize such a practice.

We decided that such a task would have to take as its primary consideration what manner of testing would be appropriate to deciding whether we were in fact operating in a contemporary mode beyond inquiry. This decision as well proved to be a question of indetermination but not inquiry. We had had the intuition for some time that we intended to proceed through the exploration of cases, which seemed to us to embody parameters of the contemporary, although we had not yet established what such parameters were and how to fit them into an overall design.

At first we thought that our cases provided satisfactory examples of crucibles of the contemporary from which we could establish determinations via a kind of comparative understanding. We later rejected this move as too methodological and more importantly not sufficiently anthropological or contemporary. It was not anthropological, we thought eventually, in that difference had received insufficient attention; it was simply posited as a given. Further, such an approach would not be contemporary in that it avoided explicitly addressing the topic of narrative, its mood and mode, appropriate to contemporary form-giving on the part of those we had chosen to study and the means by which we gave form to those studies. Said another way, we wanted to keep the tone and manner of an essay rather than a treatise. What tone and manner of an essay in the anthropology of the contemporary in the twenty-first century, however, remained to be designed and tested.

Works and Lives

We have, by working consistently with the pairing of logic and experience, learned to inhabit a second-order position that allows us to monitor our own motion while conducting inquiry, as well as assembling other salient experiments in form. We will explore two such experiments in the media of literature and painting. We take up in sequence: Salman Rushdie and the event which came to be known as an "affair"; and Gerhard Richter and the breakdown and repair in the ecology of visibility and criticism which he has constituted.

One important criterion for selection has been to focus on instances in which works and lives have brought forth some form of public response. Remembering and agreeing with John Dewey's claim that publics are not preexistent but arise when certain types of problems gain prominence, we hold that to the extent that we can identify and narrate the qualities of certain works and lives and the type and manner of responses they have occasioned, we can, without claiming scientific validity for our pursuits, introduce a set of parameters that can function to authorize further exploration.

Given what we knew about Gerhard Richter and Salman Rushdie from other engagements, our intuition of taking up cases still seemed right, but the reason to take them up, we had decided, lay in the domain of the indeterminate. After a good deal of discussion we felt confident that in quite different ways Richter and Rushdie were experimenting themselves: both on the materials they were working on and their own manner of working. Whatever else they were doing, they were constantly engaged with testing the limits of their practice. Their practice, obviously different than our own, nonetheless was clearly vocational. Painting and writing obsessed them; in their own eyes it made them who they were. Testing that vocation was an essential part of their vocation. The differences between and among their practices and our own provided the space for designing an anthropological project in and of the contemporary.

Gedankenbild

At previous stages of inquiry, Dewey's "forms-standards" concept pointed to specific types of equipment essential in the initial ordering out of which we could arrive at connections between logic and experience. Thus, for example, the studios proved to be the kind of equipment that could produce the type of pragmatic reduction appropriate to actual configurations of discordancy. We knew we needed pragmatic reduction of the experience of

Table 1 This table functioned for us as an early stage ordering device to link the terms we thought would function as parameters to the cases we anticipated using.

Crucibles of the Contemporary	Kairos	Nachleben	Pathosformel
Painting			
The novel			
Anthropology			

the present and the studio provided the space in which observations and determinations could be tested and displayed so as to begin narrative ordering.

At this stage, we were at first tempted to think of the cases as ideal types. Thus, for example, Gerhard Richter would be the example of an ideal type of rendering visible and Salman Rushdie the ideal type of finding appropriate types of rendering discursive the situation that confronted him. While this was helpful before we began the work on the cases, we realized that ideal types were not what we were after as they are used traditionally as propaedeutic to inquiry.

Consequently we thought that perhaps an initial ordering device was really a *Gedankenbild*, a "thought-image."[3] These *Gedankenbilden* provide a visibility and order of a range of terms one is considering. For us, however, they are not a prelude to inquiry but rather an aid in imagining the broad contours of a narrative structure. We are not writing fiction, although we understand that narrating the contemporary requires a disciplined set of distinctions that differ from the propositional ones appropriate to the practice and goals of inquiry.

Contemporary Design Workshop: Parameters

But victorious capitalism, since it rests on mechanical foundations, needs [spiritual] support no longer. The rosy blush of its laughing heir, the Enlightenment, also seems to be irretrievably fading, and the idea of duty in one's calling prowls about in our lives like the ghost of dead religious beliefs.

—Max Weber[4]

It is not the actual interconnection of things but the conceptual interconnection of problems which define the scope of the various sciences. A new science emerges where new problems are pursued by new methods and truths are thereby discovered which open up significant new points of view.

—Max Weber[5]

Max Weber's claim that the vocational challenge of knowledge seekers is to open up significant new points of view through working on the conceptual interconnection of problems is one we accept. We do not follow Weber, however, in thinking that the disciplines of existing sciences are totally constrained by the conditions of modernity. A century after Weber's sober precepts, we think that there is more than one path forward.

Our project has been to identify the parameters of the contemporary as a mode of observation and a mode of existence. In order to do so, and since we are no longer engaged in Deweyan inquiry, we no longer require standards to guide us; rather the task is to identify and test parameters. What is a parameter? A parameter is

> a fact or circumstance that restricts how something is done or what can be done; a variable value that, when it changes, gives another different but related mathematical expression from a limited series of such expressions.

Parameters are useful in delimiting domains. They are vital in establishing the criteria for identifying cases as well as parsing their similarities and differences. Parameters are principles of restriction. We introduce five into our overall design: authorship, metrics, moods, cases, and interpretive analytics.

1. Authorship

To the extent we gain traction in this undertaking we will have completed the identification of a series that we feel is essential to an anthropology of the contemporary. That series is *warranted assertibility, vindication*, and *authorization*. The first term is arrived at through the process of inquiry. The second is arrived at through finding a form for ethical conduct appropriate to the practices one is seeking to instantiate. The third term is arrived at only once one has become aware of, practiced, and reflected on the critical strengths and limitations of the first two terms.

That being said, each of the three terms might well be at play in the work of arriving at a satisfactory form of the others. Thus, the process of inquiry needs to be narrated if its warranted assertions are to be shared, contested, and enriched. The process of arriving at a vindicatory subject position rather than a reactive self-justificatory one is made possible in part and depending on the circumstances by the completion of a stage of successful inquiry and, as in the case of Seneca, the practice of a form of narration that sustains the mode of subjectivation for which one is striving. Nonetheless, although each of the three terms may be at play in a particular practice, one of the terms is primed in each instance. Furthermore, even if the terms constitute a series that is reiterative, its genesis follows a certain order: warrant, vindication, authorship.

2. Metrics

We have previously used Aristotle's term *horos* to indicate a standard or measure which is specific to a person in a situation. Standards assist us in the search for the mean in situations. With our transition from situations of inquiry toward cases of contemporary practices, we pay special attention to breakdown and repair of forms. Our observation remains oriented to excesses, deficiencies, and means, made possible by the clarification that the practice of our ethical fourfold affords.

The use of metrics has previously served to guide and constrain inquiry and we have confidence that they can function as well to guide and constrain an anthropological mode of observation for the contemporary. After inquiry, however, metrics, like standards, will have to be designed to function differently than they did during inquiry where we deployed them to identify the overall goals of a practice and to use the standard to gauge ethical sufficiency or insufficiency. At that stage the metrics we found fruitful were prosperity, amelioration, and flourishing.

Reconstruction, Remediation

Dewey's terms provided the means to move from the level of situational breakdown to propositions concerning the actual. To move beyond the actual, however, requires a different logic and a different type of experience. It also entails the introduction of a type of discourse that typifies the general situation in which the microbreakdowns occur. In order to confront the troubles, deficiencies, and excesses of macrosituations Dewey introduced the term *reconstruction*. Reconstruction, we remember, consists in

> nothing less than the work of developing, of forming, of producing (in the literal sense of that word) the intellectual instrumentalities which will progressively direct inquiry into the deeply and inclusively human—that is to say moral—facts of the present scene and situation.[6]

Having conducted extensive inquiry ourselves, and having developed an elaborate set of intellectual instrumentalities to aid that inquiry, we concluded that more than the intellectual was required to carry out such a task.

Power inequalities, institutional arrangements, trained incapacities, the dead end of competence, the allergy to light of this depraved animal, among a long list of other impediments, calls to mind Max Weber's comment that the rosy bloom of the Enlightenment had long since faded away.

The results of our inquiry, the configurations of the actual, persuaded us that today reconstruction was at best a utopian horizon. Lowering the scope of the macro to a more manageable scale, we shifted our hopes from reconstruction to remediation.[7] *Remediation* has a double sense: it refers to a problem to be redressed and a shift of medium or technical means in order to address it. Operating at this pragmatic middle range we found that remediation frequently proved useful in advancing our inquiry, although ultimately it too ran into real-world obstacles.

As we move from the process of inquiry and its task of producing warrantable propositions about specific situations, we are confronted with a possibility that the type of breakdowns to be considered as contemporary are of a different order than confronting those of inquiry, or even judgment in a simple sense. It is here that we have found useful Foucault's brief detour during his lectures on the care of the self to the term *sōzein*. We take up the term in the senses of repairing, protecting, and making whole. The term has opened up a different space of affect and consequently attention to how one could take up a different range of breakdowns.

Foucault identifies the Greek term *sōzein* as once playing a central cultural role; he also argued that it contributed centrally to the form of ancient philosophy. Remembering once again that a term is a word + concept + referent, Foucault provides in two short pages a list of the term's semantic scope.[8] The term has a range of meanings in ancient Greek: to guard and to protect, in both literal and figurative senses; to exonerate or defend in juridical setting; as well as insure well-being, of a subject, something, or a collectivity.[9] *Sōzein* as a term has functioned to make visible a conceptual interconnection of problems whose existence is unquestionable, but whose entry into the play of knowledge and truth has been excluded, or blocked.

Although obviously the cultural and historical setting in which *sōzein* functioned is long gone and without invoking a general theory of human nature, we have found it extremely useful as a way of identifying concepts and referents to which the word might well apply today. Hence, we are not proposing a theory of care, or putting it forward like Heidegger as an *Existenzial*; rather we are deploying it from our experience of inquiry itself, but more importantly from the problem of what to do after inquiry.[10]

Weber after all argued that the things themselves were not ultimately the real for those seeking the truth and in fact could constitute blinders as to other possibilities, other forms of life. We follow Weber here in his advice to proceed with the conceptual interconnection of problems in the hope that significant new points of view could be opened up.

Repair

We venture that there are significant new points of view that might be opened up that depend on inquiry but are not determined by inquiry. Such points of view require minimally recognition that inquiry requires breakdown. Such breakdown, in experience and in situations, may not be reconstructable and may not be remediable, or one may seek an activity other than indefinite efforts at remediation. We unexpectedly found a term that could characterize the action of observation and intervention which we sought in the transition to a contemporary mode in which to take up breakdowns in form: *repair.*

We use *repair* in three senses: its older meaning draws on an active sense of motion, to repair to a place; we recognize a transient modality of the verb in which a subject takes itself as the object and destination of repair. We also use it to indicate the manner in which prior breakdowns will be observed, with a sense that remedy is unlikely, but that some things from prior breakdowns are worth preserving and of bringing forward with motion. Thirdly, we use it in the sense that such motion is guided, that one makes one's way with guides, and that one has aids available to which one may repair.[11]

3. Mood

We propose that one way of accommodating an essential pluralism of points of view, without entering into a fruitless battle for dominance, is to shift from the warrantable ordering to that of narrative. We have identified four main points of view that in the spirit of Kenneth Burke will allow us, with a certain latitude, to facilitate our explorations of how to proceed. This schema, while initially providing clear distinctions of types, also provides for the possibility of multiple recombinations yielding variants.

Given our choice to privilege narrative, and given our emphasis on points of view, Gérard Genette's term *mood* suits our purposes. *Mood* for Genette is the

> name given to different forms of the verb that are used to affirm more or less the same thing in question and to express . . . the different points of view from which the life or the action is looked at.[12]

The four moods we have picked out are tragedy, comedy, irony, and pathos. We have posed the question to ourselves whether all four of these moods can lead to an anthropology of the contemporary. We put this question forward as a genuine question. It is genuine in the sense that as far as we know almost no one has posed this question in this way and hence answering it definitely would be premature. Our initial hypothesis is that only two of these modes are suited to function in a mode that opens a path to the contemporary.

Drawing on the distinction that Foucault elaborated from Kant between *Gemüt* and *Geist,* we argue that the tragic position holds that *Geist* in our history is so totally dominant that any proposal that *Gemüt* can alter it in a fundamental fashion is delusional. That is to say that the role of *Gemüt* is to think about *Geist* and thereby courageously pose the configurations of the actual as limit conditions. Theodore Adorno in his *Minima Moralia: Reflections from Damaged Life* exemplified the tragic mood in his finale:

> The only philosophy which can be responsibly practiced in the face of despair is the attempt to contemplate all things as they would present themselves from the standpoint of redemption. Knowledge has no light but that shed on the world by redemption: all else is reconstruction, mere technique. Perspectives must be fashioned that displace and estrange the world, reveal it to be, with its rifts and crevices, as indigent and distorted as it will appear one day in the messianic light. To gain such perspectives without velleity or violence, entirely from felt contact with its objects—this alone is the task of thought.[13]

The ironic mood in a sense reverses the relations of *Geist* and *Gemüt*. Taking science studies and Bruno Latour as its most distinguished practitioner, concerning science the *Geist* seems to have almost no role at all in determining and limiting the range of self-affectation that is open.

Latour and Woolgar in their classic monograph *Laboratory Life* set up their scene and mood in an ironic manner:

> When an anthropological observer enters the field, one of his most fundamental preconceptions is that he might eventually be able to make sense of the observations and notes which he records. . . . For a total newcomer to the laboratory, we can imagine that his first encounter with his subjects would severely jeopardize such faith. . . . What are these people doing? What are they talking about? . . . Why is everybody whispering? What part is played by the animals who squeak incessantly in the ante-rooms? But for our partial familiarity with some aspects of scientific activity and our ability to draw upon

a body of common sense assumptions, a flood of nonsensical impressions would follow the formulation of these questions. Perhaps these animals are being processed for eating. . . . Are the heated debates in front of the blackboard part of some gambling contest?[14]

Of course, as the development of actor-network theory would go on to propose the range of affectation that is open to actants, human and otherwise, consists entirely and uniquely of one type of action, which ultimately is a kind of mechanics in its insistence that all phenomena can be explained by a micro- and macrophysics of action.[15] That is to say that ultimately there is neither *Geist* nor *Gemüt* in this position.

As Steven Shapin commented in his acerbic review of Latour's methodological manifesto *Science in Action*, "Following Scientists Around,"

"Networks" are heterogeneous in their composition. They contain entities we are accustomed to call "things" as well as those we are used to designate as "people." Anything can be an "actant" or an "actor" in technoscientific networks. Latour's erosion of the conventional boundaries separating politics from science is predicated upon the insistence that objects and non-human entities as well as people are political beings. Things belong to the study of political order as much as human agents.[16]

The comedic mood maintains a relation of both *Geist* and *Gemüt*. In that sense, it is at least a potential candidate for narratives of the contemporary. We are using *comedy* in the older sense of temporary resolution. Such a mood recognizes that things break down all the time but equally that there are momentary or short-lived reconciliations. In this sense, *Geist* understood as macrodeterminations both historical and subjective are always in play. There is, however, in this mood a constant emphasis on self-affectation, often delusional and thereby comic, but nonetheless even delusional action may lead to reconciliation and repair. The comedic, one could hold, never loses sight of the need for and availability of practices of *sōzein* up and down the scale from love to the law. The trope of repair is prominent, in the sense of movement to sites of refuge and temporary reconciliation. That being said, these repairs are always vulnerable to larger forces and need to be rebuilt.

The mood of pathos turns on breakdown and repair leading to more breakdown and repair. It certainly takes *Geist* into account as a dominant vector providing major determinations of situations and action. The mood of pathos, however, and this is what gives it its specificity, requires self-affectation, which is not delusional, in the comedic sense, but at least in its more accomplished forms recognizes both the necessity and finitude of taking up and testing whatever margins of freedom exist under particular conditions. This is not reconciliation, again in the comedic sense, but rather a mode of testing limits, resisting resignation, and seeking maturity. The mood of pathos, as with the comedic, seeks motion toward a near future. This orientation is unlike the mood of the tragic which seeks a far future and unlike the ironic whose future is always the same. The near future to which the mood of pathos looks requires a veridictional practice.

4. Contemporary Cases

Given the determinations of metrics and mood, it follows that designs on the contemporary is not experimental per se in the search for warranted assertibility, but rather is an issue of judging the power and richness of attempts (our own and others') to render visible and sayable situations. It follows that we would pay careful second-order attention to cases in which repair, *sōzein*, and design are brought into a relationship, one with the other. Within such cases we will pay attention to the *kairos*, the turning point or opportune moment; *Nachleben*, that which survives or endures after the breakdown in forms; and *Pathosformel*, how particular *Nachleben* can be made to endure and the forms that can be invented and given after breakdown.

Kairos

Turning points are an essential standard within situations insofar as motion and unexpected ramifications seem to be essential to any narrative both of pathos and comedy, but more importantly of our experience of attempting to think about the contemporary and to give it form. This claim does not mean that motion is always achieved, but only that even in situations of stasis it appears possible to those involved that there should be motion. Such motion, one could say, is precisely the contemporary relation of the *Gemüt* in relation to the *Geist*.

Nachleben

We hold that there is no escape from historicity, but we also hold that history is no longer the fixed site of significance (so much for the ironic and the tragic). That being said, fragments of past forms are absolutely salient in this mood and mode for *sōzein*, for repair, for assemblage, for narrative, in a word, for the contemporary (as opposed to the high modern). There is a recognition that past forms had something to teach and had broken down. Consequently, attempting to recuperate them whole is both futile and delusional because they were constructed for particular problems which are no longer the same, but on the other hand are not so radically "other" that there is nothing to learn from them and the past per se is inescapable in multiple ways that need to be addressed. This can be taken up in a tragic and ironic mode in which the past in fact dominates, or in a minor mode in which Aristotle and Seneca can to a degree offer us terms drawn from their logic and experience and which need to be taken up pragmatically and worked over, but nonetheless are not totally foreign. In that sense they have a *Nachleben*.

They are not mere survivals as the term is sometimes misleadingly translated. Rather, as we approach the conceptual interconnection of problems and not of things, we have developed a mode of appropriation, second-order observation intervention (*Betrachtung*), which seems to allow us to appreciate how thinking took place and was active in the past and to what degree it "survives" as aids for us today. That mode of survival can be literal, but is not metaphorical or analogical. Rather, it can be equipmental, terminological, narratological, etc. One can observe past crucibles of experimentation and experience using them as *Gedankenbilden*, that is to say, hence, a kind of extended *paraskeuē*, but not analogy, for approaching the contemporary as both object and objective.

The crucible of Seneca and Lucilius' epistolary practice is not severed from us, even though it cannot endure without transformation. James Ker helped us to see the historical conditions under which this form took shape and hence given that we live under radically different historical conditions but ones in which there is a deficit of forms, particularly those devoted to *philia* in the philosophic sense, the possibility of the invention of other forms was buttressed. We could repair, as it were, to Seneca and Lucilius knowing that we would need to venture forward on our own with whatever equipment we could take from them. In fact, it was not letter writing that we decided upon but studios, etc.

The epistolary form constituted the *Gemüt* for working over and through the discordances of the actual. It included *sōzein*, repair, attention to *kairos*, and Seneca's somewhat surprising recuperation of other schools of philosophy (*Nachleben*). He made them function as *paraskeuē* in the quest for a form, which turned out to be, we can see, a *Pathosformel*. It provided some solace through thinking and form-giving, perhaps informed by the need for self-affectation but not reducible to the level of affect although its aim ultimately was to affect the affect. The affect Seneca privileged was the Stoic *ataraxia*, which we have argued is neither available nor desirable today. Hence, the *Nachleben* provides help of a specific sort including an awareness, and hence the pathos, that that form is no longer available as a form.

Pathosformel

What we have learned so far is simultaneously that the quest for form follows science (in which further formal experimentation has been normalized through the article, the conference, the journal, etc.). We have also learned that others have sought forms combining elements of veridiction and self-affectation. Such forms were created to address discordances and breakdowns and ultimately however long they endured at some point were felt to be inadequate to the next *kairos*. Attempts to reconstruct, or remediate these breakdowns or turning points have taken the form of the history of ideas or the assertion of values, which seem to provide stable solutions, at least discursively. For those of us seeking repair, having come to the conclusion through experience and experimentation that reconstruction and remediation are inadequate and unsatisfactory for the problem at hand, the challenge therefore is to find form for the *Nachleben* of previous forms, knowing full well that at best it is a temporary solution. But this insight in no way obviates the urgency of the quest; it only renders it in a mood of pathos.

5. Interpretive Analytics

In an addendum to Foucault's first lecture of the 1982–83 lectures at the Collège de France, *Le gouvernement de soi et des autres*, which existed in his prepared text but which he did not read to his audience we find a set of precepts ("rules of action") of stunning power.[17] Following his advice on how to respond to the reproaches that one is certain to receive—don't accept the opening gambit of your opponents' attacks or you are lost, even if you win the polemic—Foucault preceded, in one of those white-hot torrents of prose which he rarely allowed to be made public, to lay out the following precepts, or rules of action.

For us, these precepts are also *paraskeuē*, ready-at-hand devices and defenses. It is in this double register of general rules of action, as well as ever-present equipment, that one might qualify them as a component of both a posterior and an anterior analytics, which we will join under the term *interpretive analytics*.

The precepts are as follows:[18]

There are above all its immediately apparent "negative," negativist aspects:

1. A historicizing negativism, since it involves replacing a theory of knowledge, power, or the subject with the analysis of historically determinate practices.

2. A nominalist negativism, since it involves replacing universals like madness, crime and sexuality with the analysis of experiences which constitute singular historical forms.

3. A negativism with a nihilist tendency, if by this we understand a form of reflection which, instead of indexing practices to systems of values which allow them to be assessed, inserts these systems of values in the interplay of arbitrary but intelligible practices.[19]

Anterior to inquiry or narration, one is well-advised to keep the following questions and guidelines available for guidance and rectification:[20]

1. The question of historicism is: what have been and may be the effects of historical analysis in the field of historical thought?

2. The question of nominalism is: what have been the effects of nominalist criticism in the analyses of culture, knowledge, institutions and political structures?

3. The question of nihilism is: what have been and what may be the effects of nihilism in the acceptance and transformation of systems of values?

To the objections that postulate the disqualification of nihilism/nominalism/historicism, we should try to reply by undertaking a historicist, nominalist, nihilist analysis of this current. By this I mean: not construct this form of thought in its universal systematic character and justify it in terms of truth or moral value, but rather to seek to know how the constitution and development of this critical game, this form of thought, was possible.[21]

The first line of Aristotle's *Posterior analytics* reads, "All instruction given or received by way of argument proceeds from pre-existent knowledge."[22] If one substitutes the term *narration* for *argument* one would be approaching the mode and mood of the contemporary. Both the *preexisting knowledge* (which we call the *actual* and which is the product of inquiry) and *instruction* (which for us includes testing, experiment, *Bildung*, and the search for a form) are indispensable in how we understand our project. The references to Aristotle are intended as pragmatic and not in any way an attempt to resurrect an old form any more than our understanding of logic was pragmatic and not in any way an attempt to resurrect an older form of logic such as that of Hegel.

In that light, we intend to take up and find a form to narrate our cases by:

1   Being attentive to the historicity of those involved both in their own self-understanding and experimentation and our own, second-order observations of their practices. Given the omnipresence of history in modernity (either as present or as negation), we are attentive to how historicity is taken up once "History," capital H, is abandoned or excluded.

2   Approaching a case in the manner we are exploring entails beginning with a nominalist perspective on universals or theories. It entails undertaking the exploration and subsequent ordering of experiences and experiments that others have put to their own tests; we proceed in a second-order manner once again in the hope that each of these cases can be made to render the *historically singular forms* produced. Attaining some grasp on that level of singularity, however, is not our stopping point or goal. Our experiment currently consists in multiplying such cases of historically singular forms so as to ascertain what generality, if any, we can discern among and between them.

3   Approaching a case in the manner we are exploring entails beginning with a nihilist perspective on value systems used as guides to action or analysis. Once again, the goal of such an undertaking is not to inscribe nihilism as a grid or goal but as a precept thereby opening up an exploration of the cases we have chosen to make studies of in which those concerned struggle with freeing themselves from the dominant value systems of their day—and are frequently reproached for doing so—without however striving to inscribe a thoroughly new system in its place. Rather, they, like us, are attentive to practices of testing modal alterations and the moods in which they can be cast.

FOUR

The Rushdie Affair: Truth and Conduct

A man who sets out to make himself up is taking on the Creator's role, according to one way of seeing things; he's unnatural, a blasphemer, an abomination
of abominations. From another angle, you could see pathos in him, heroism in
his struggle, in his willingness to risk: not all mutants survive. Or, consider him
socio-politically: most migrants learn, and can become disguises. Our own false
descriptions to counter the falsehoods invented about us, concerns for reasons of
security our secret selves.

—Salman Rushdie, *The Satanic Verses*[1]

On September 26, 1988, Viking Press in London published Salman Rushdie's fourth novel, *The Satanic Verses*. The novel was banned soon after in
several countries (India, Pakistan, South Africa, Bangladesh, and Sudan)
and subsequently on February 14th of the following year, was censured
as blasphemous, its author denounced as an apostate and condemned to
death by the Supreme Leader of Iran, Ayatollah Khomeini, along with Rushdie's editors and publishers.

The conception and creation of the novel was a turning point in Rushdie's writing, marking his taking leave of historical architectures within
which to frame his narratives. Rushdie had risen to prominence as a writer
in the early 1980s with two books renarrating the recent past of India and
Pakistan. *Midnight's Children* (1981) shifted the historical and political
frame through which to understand Independence and partition of British
India. Rushdie drew on the fabulist forms of storytelling on which he had
grown up, in order to transform the available national epic of freedom and
through which to narrate the intertwining of the historical trajectory of the
nation and the lives of those born under the sign of Independence. He has
his protagonist, Saleem Sinai, open the narrative:

I had been mysteriously handcuffed to history, my destinies indissolubly chained to those of my country. For the next three decades, there was to be no escape. Soothsayers had prophesied me, newspapers celebrated my arrival, politicos ratified my authenticity. I was left entirely without a say in the matter.[2]

Sinai's narrative, of himself and India, both binds their intertwined histories while also disrupting fatalist narratives of freedom, as well as tragic narratives of loss. One could say *Gemüt* and *Geist* are held in a comic ratio.

His third novel, *Shame* (1983), charts the political and ethical effects of passions in three families in a town called Q, which is almost Pakistan.[3] The novel fits within the parameters of the moral fable, where characters within the family—who stand in for a shameless class created under but not only by colonialism—are tested and whose petty, self-serving actions admit of judgments along an axis of excess and deficiency, judgments performed with authority by Rushdie as intervening narrator, again within a comic mood.

Midnight's Children and *Shame* used historical frames but were not historical novels per se. Their effects and effectiveness—the former won the Booker Prize and the latter the prize for best translation in Farsi awarded by the Iranian government!—came in part from their capacity to narrate a different actuality of the life of new nations and of the lives within them.

Rushdie's Indeterminations

In *The Satanic Verses* Rushdie dispenses with a historical frame. To a degree the novel marked a reentry for Rushdie into the present, into the discordance of experience and the indetermination of writing as part of *technē tou biou*.

Pragmatically viewed, the novel was a response to an indetermination in the present: How to write about religion as someone who does not believe in revealed truth? One way is through culture, or through traditions as sets of practices within which to make sense of religious beliefs, even if one does not believe them oneself. One could call this a modern anthropological position. As indicated previously, culture as an anthropological device has arguably blocked thinking about the breakdowns and repairs which occasion thinking *for* the one doing the thinking—in this instance, the problem of religious claims to truth in the afterlife of modernity for those seeking to inquire into the problematization of modernity.

Rushdie adds a second dimension to his indetermination: How to take up claims to revealed truth for those whose cultural milieu has shifted or been transformed? How to think about claims to revealed truth within contexts of the cultural multiple, without recourse to stabilized reproduction of cultural norms?[4] Rushdie was searching for a form to work through the multiple experiences of migration, cultural and historical motion, and the breakdowns in self-understanding that accompany such motion. What is striking about the novel and what distinguishes it from his prior two successes is that themes of movement, cultural identification and change, what he has called an "ethic of impurity," are tackled through confusions of revealed truth and man-made fictions. How to take cultures and cultural change seriously if one does not know how to engage with fundamental claims to truth within those cultures?

> It was clear to me as someone who doesn't have a formal belief in religion that when a prophet says that an archangel appears to him and gives him the word of God, then I am unable to take it literally. On the other hand I'm also unable to dismiss it because it is clear he's not lying.[5]

In sum, Rushdie characterizes *The Satanic Verses* in two distinct ways: on the one hand as an attempt to produce a secular confrontation with revelation, and to explore the parameters of cultural change in that confrontation, for those people like himself who hear this indetermination *as a problem*.

He described the problem a year before finishing the book, in the following terms,

> The book is about angels and devils and about how it's very difficult to establish ideas of morality in a world which has become so uncertain that it is difficult to even agree on what is happening. When one can't agree on a description of reality, it is very hard to agree on whether that reality is good or evil, right or wrong. . . . Angels and devils are becoming confused ideas. What I think the novel is also about is the act of migration, and of hybridization, of the way in which people become combinations.[6]

At the level of *technē*, the novel, he wrote to himself in a notebook, "must perform the crisis it describes."[7] The *performance* of a description—a description of an encounter and confusion of the sacred and profane, as well as of the encounters of subjects changed through their descriptions of one another—itself operates at a second order. As Rushdie observed:

I did not want to write a kind of sociologically based fiction about how terrible it is today for black people in England. I wanted to write a novel which at its most fundamental level is about metamorphosis—the nature of it, the process by which it happens, its effect on the metamorphosed self and on the world around it, and its link with the act of travelling.[8]

We will take up this performance, second order as it already is, at a second order of observation: an observation of the experience and effects of the writing—as *technē* for Rushdie, how it circulates for others, including ourselves as anthropologists, and the aftereffects it creates.

Propositions

Rushdie sets out neither to write a historical fiction, nor to write a sociological portrait of the discordant actuality of migrants' position and marginality within metropoles. His effort to grasp an indetermination in experience at a conjuncture in the present (London ca. 1983–88) began with a story that had stayed with him for twenty years. For Rushdie to be operating within the domain of indetermination it is important to recognize that his starting point for the novel is a historical event in Islam, one whose significance is disputed and whose significance for the writer comes from its irresolution. This irresolution, we will argue, marks the pathos of the text—tragically read as comedy or irony—as well as the events that followed, also read alternately as tragedy and comedy.

A major inception point of the novel is that while the chain of transmission (*isnad*) of authorized statements or acts (*hadith*) attributed to the Prophet Mohammad (570–632 CE) is incomplete, there exist numerous accounts within commentaries on the Qur'an of an incident that came to be known as the incident of satanic verses.[9]

In London, at the Institute for Contemporary Arts, the day after the publication of the novel (September 27, 1988), Rushdie explained the historical theological source of his work's genesis:

I suppose the novel began in a number of places, one of which is the incident from which the title of the book comes, which I suppose I've known about for twenty years. When I was studying Islamic History as one of my papers of my final year at college [Cambridge], I came across this amazing incident in which the Prophet Mohammed, it is said, flirted with—or at least God had said—flirted with the idea of tolerating the three most famous and lucrative pagan goddesses of Mecca as acceptable at the level of archangels, as kind of intermediary beings. And there were verses of the Qur'an which accepted them, which said that they were exalted birds and their intercession was greatly to be desired. And then, at some later moment, Mohammed repudiated these verses and said that the devil had appeared to him disguised as the archangel (Gabriel). And these had been Satanic verses, which had to be expelled from the Qur'an and were to be replaced by new verses which said that these creatures were completely unimportant, that God wanted nothing to do with them.[10]

Within Islamic exegetical literature, the debates around this episode, the acceptance, rejection, and possible significance of it have come to turn on issues of both its legitimacy within traditions of commentary and its meaning. The first writer to record the incident was Ibn Ishaq (704–770 CE), author of the first biography of Prophet Mohammad, on whose authority later exegetes such as Tabari (838–923 CE) repeated the episode.

There have been three ways in which this episode has been viewed: (a) rejected as fabrication; (b) accepted and explained away as insignificant; or (c) accepted and requiring interpretation. Rushdie took the latter option.

Scholars such as Ibn Hasan Tabarsi (1073–1153 CE) in his commentaries on the Qur'an, worked through many possible explanations and interpretations of the episode, ranging from psychological weakness exploited by Satan to lexical ambiguity.[11] Tabarsi's final suggestion as to how to interpret the episode is to understand it as a test by God of human desire. Ibrahim al-Kurani (1616–97) provides the following reasoning for accepting the legitimacy of the episode and to interpret it as a test:

(1) To reject the story is to reject the authority of true and authentic tradition. This cannot be right. Again, it seems to run counter to the express statement in the Qur'an that Satan has tampered with the messages of every prophet and God has intervened to cancel the false and establish the true. (2) It cannot be explained away by asserting Satan himself was the speaker. That is a downright contradiction of the Qur'an, as has just been said, and the tradition in question shows plainly that the prophet himself spoke, because he repeated the words to Gabriel in good faith, believing that they had come to him through Gabriel. (3) Thus the story must be true, and it can be shown that satanic suggestion is a means by which God tests men's hearts.[12]

Rushdie took seriously the general point, which one could take up in religious or nonreligious terms, that orthodoxies and cultural practices of truth emerge out of tests and turning points, only later to be structured as determinate, but which retain questions that prompted the test.

Nachleben

Rushdie is modern and modernist. The breakdown that occasions his reflection on the story of satanic verses is of the confrontation of realities that lack an ordering principle.

The novel was read by some people as blasphemous, a denigration of the veracity of the Qur'an. Divine revelation was figured as a psychological breakdown and was considered to have been mocked by a secular humanist. Others rendered the work exemplary of a right and freedom to write, a right which was under threat by a coordinated Islamic campaign. The afterlife of what came to be understood as an affair could and, we will argue, *should* be read as a test and particularly as a test for anthropological observers of the affair and of the manner in which it was structured and played out.

We thus interpret the polemic as an institutionally created event, rather than as a consequence of the specific content of the novel. At a second order of observation, it is possible to ask how judgments—Rushdie's own judgments about the experience and effects of his writing, as well as others' judgments about the effects of the novel—were made, which is to say, the modes in which the text was rendered actual.

In order to pose this question of the manner in which the performance of the test was actualized, we draw on extant observations, heuristics, and analyses of Rushdie himself insofar as his accounts of himself are the materials we, anthropologists and other commentators, have to draw on to ask how the event was constituted, how it functioned as an affair, and through what modes determinations (of the actual) were made about it. This work enables us to prepare for a contemporary narration.

Although Rushdie as novelist found a different mode of engaging the present—he did not seek to reactualize either the history of Islam, or the experience of immigration in 1980s Britain per se —as anthropologists of the contemporary, our task is first to observe and move through the actuality of the affair, in order to narrate its afterlife.

In our movement from the actual to the contemporary, we ask how this actuality of the affair could be taken up by us in a mood of pathos, with attention to a contemporary metric of repair, narrating the afterlife of the affair?

These parameters do not negate, overcome, or jettison the problematic of the modern—the *problem* of legitimate self-assertion in Blumenberg's specific sense, of the practice of *techne* after the breakdown of divine order—which exists both in Rushdie's text as a second-order description of a crisis and of the manner in which many read, responded to, and critiqued the text as an event. Rather, through these parameters we are attempting to forge a position of observation in which to recast the movement and effect of the affair that one could narrate as a ratio of breakdown and repair.

Instances, Concepts, Problems: Labinar Fall 2012

Stavrianakis co-organized Rabinow's fall 2012 experiment in graduate pedagogy, known as the "Labinar."[13] A key design challenge of the Labinar is that forms need to be invented within the university so as to encourage both the reduction of student performance of what they already know and to encourage collaborative work on instances, concepts, and problems, perhaps connected to but not identical to those at play in graduate students' thesis work.

The fall Labinar was organized around the theme of media and veridiction. We sought to investigate within the space and time frame of the semester, and through work in collaborative groups, how a range of media create and circulate veridictional claims today. We outlined a plan for the semester which could guide the ongoing and changing shape of how and what the collaborative groups would work on.

The semester had three phases: work on instances, on concepts, and on forms for problems. The first phase asked groups to proliferate instances where experiences of media and veridiction were at stake and were troubling in some capacity for those identifying the instances. The second phase was oriented to identifying and honing concepts that would help to determine aspects of the instances under consideration. Thirdly, the challenge of the semester was to mobilize instances and concepts in order to name a problem of the general theme of media and veridiction, and to give a form to the problem named. Moreover, we sought to reflect on the manner in which anthropological inquiry can both observe and participate in such media.

A series of small groups began to proliferate clusters of instances where troubled experiences with and in media had provoked questions of truth, conduct, and judgment. A first group, catalyzed by the question Rabinow and Stavrianakis had previously posed—of how, when, and why anthropologists exit the field—took up the figure of the whistleblower as a figure who is required to change position (leave a situation, speak outside of an organization, to a different center of authority) in order to make a truth claim. A second group focused on Internet-enabled labor technologies, the proliferation of their uses, and the creation of countertechnologies for the surveillance of these labor technologies.

Stavrianakis participated in a group which was exploring a set of interconnected instances which had emerged in mid-September, as the seminar got underway: reports of the killing of the US ambassador J. Christopher Stevens and others in Benghazi, Libya, on September 11, 2012; the connection of the event to a YouTube video "The Innocence of Muslims" first uploaded in June 2012; reports by the Associated Press that the murder of Stevens was part of "mob rioting" caused by the film; further global demonstrations against the film that followed the September 11, 2012 event; and the satirization of the global demonstrations against the video by *Charlie Hebdo*, the French weekly (*hebdo*) which specializes in that genre.[14]

Instance

Stavrianakis had been intrigued with the instance of *Charlie Hebdo's* response to the global Islamic protests, as a site where a vocation and testing seemed to be at play. In part this was because in November 2011 the *Charlie Hebdo* office had been firebombed after it published a special issue, titled *Charia Hebdo*, "To fittingly celebrate the victory of the Islamist Ennahda party in Tunisia." A smiling Mohammad promised the reader "a hundred lashes if you don't die of laughter." It seemed to Stavrianakis that what the weekly magazine was doing in September 2012 could not be understood in terms of a "right" to satirize—which framed the majority of critics' and defenders' responses. Such a freedom and right do not answer the question, why satirize at that moment in the way they did?

The cover of the September 19, 2012, edition depicts what could be read as a Hasidic rabbi pushing an imam, in a wheelchair, with the pair concordantly exclaiming: "Don't mock us!" The image is set up as a mock poster of a sequel to a popular French film from the previous year, *Intouchables* (Untouchables)—the true story of a wealthy, physically disabled risk taker, who lost his wife in an accident and whose experience of the world is transformed when he hires a young Muslim ex-convict as his caregiver. As promotional materials rendered the story, "their bond proves the power and omniscience that love and friendship can hold over all social and economic differences."

One available answer as to what was happening in the September 19th edition of *Charlie Hebdo* was that the purpose of cartoons in general, and of cartoons about Mohammad featured within the edition were, like the *Innocence of Muslims*, aimed at insulting Muslims.[15] This answer seemed limited and reductive, and to pay little or no attention to timing and specificity of the gesture. What was the object being shown? Not something about Islam per se, but rather something about the manner in which a field of affect around Islam is narrated as part of global political events today.

Inside the magazine, the creation of the *Innocence of Muslims* was satirized under the pun, "Le film qui embrase le monde musulman" ("the film which ignites the Muslim world.") *Innocence* and its after-effects were reportrayed as a behind-the-scenes shot from Godard's *Le Mépris* (Contempt), with an actor playing Mohammad standing in for a naked Brigitte Bardot and an exasperated and disgusted Godard looking on.

The US State Department explained the attack in Benghazi by way of a narrative of "Muslim rage" over the film *Innocence of Muslims*. The Associated Press reported on September 11, 2012: "A mob enraged by a film ridiculing Islam's prophet killed the U.S. ambassador to Libya and three other Americans in a fiery attack on the U.S. Consulate in Benghazi."[16] This narrative was shown subsequently to be spurious.

In a different reading of the September 19th drawings, *Charlie Hebdo* was satirizing how reactions (ranging from peaceful demonstrations to serious violence) to a film that aimed to propagandize against Islam were normalized by participants and observers, as part of narratives about Muslims and Islam, specifically through tropes of conflagration. This matters with respect to the bombing of the magazine's offices from the previous year. On the one hand the US Department of State narrative that "Muslim rage" could possibly explain the political events in Benghazi is undermined; on the other hand, the cartoons carry a mocking, antagonist gesture against the violence perpetrated in Paris the previous year.

To bring our instances into a common frame we posed a grid of questions:

1 What is the mode of subjectivation for those making speech acts in and about polemical situations?
2 How is the mode of subjectivation and the significance of the object tied to its mode of transmission?
3 What is an anthropological judgment about the situations in which polarized and overdetermined objects circulate?

The first question had intrigued Stavrianakis when thinking about the editorial decision made by *Charlie Hebdo* to publish a set of cartoons about the YouTube film and subsequent reactions, in the aftermath of the global demonstrations. The second question was appropriate to the core issue of form and circulation. To gain clarity about the third question required more conceptual work.

Modes of Judgment: Context, Critique, Test

As in heresiology, polemics sets itself the task of determining the intangible point of dogma, the fundamental and necessary principle that the adversary has neglected, ignored or transgressed; and it denounces this negligence as a moral failing; at the root of the error, it finds passion, desire, interest, a whole series of weaknesses and inadmissible attachments that establish it as culpable.

—Michel Foucault[17]

Although no anthropologists had taken up the incident of *Charlie Hebdo*, either immediately in the wake of the 2012 cartoons, or after the episode from the previous year, the topic of cartoons portraying Mohammad arose previously around the decision of the Danish newspaper *Jyllens-Posten* to pose a question to forty cartoonists and to publish their responses: How do you see Mohammad?

The episode from September 2005 generated significant anthropological engagement, including a monograph by Jeanne Favret-Saada, *Comment produire une crise mondiale: Avec douze petits dessins*; a volume of debates between Talal Asad, Wendy Brown, Saba Mahmood and Judith Butler *Is Critique Secular?*; and an article by Webb Keane in *Public Culture*, "Freedom and Blasphemy: On Indonesian Press Bans and Danish Cartoons," on the semiotic ideology at play in the decision to publish the cartoons, and the effect of this ideology in structuring the incomprehension of Europeans to the anger of some Muslims about the publication of the cartoons.

We characterized the situation of instances in 2012 and of the cartoons from 2005 as polemical. A situation of polemic is one in which a speaker proceeds in antagonistic discourse with a privilege and legitimacy which she refuses to question, and which the opponent is denied in advance. How then to think about anthropological modes of observation and judgment within situations structured as polemical?

Favret-Saada's book and the volume by Asad et alia, alongside Keane's essay were exemplary of what we decided were two main forms of anthropological judgment within polemical situations: contextualization, in Favret-Saada's case and evaluation in the case of the others. In Favret-Saada's deft hands, contextualization functioned as a way of making the publication of the cartoons explicable by the multiplication of variables (historical, cultural, political); the specification of factors (timing, persons involved) and the relation of factors and variables to episodes and events.

Evaluative modes of judgment turned most explicitly on the identification of the operation of ideology and the connection of the function of ideology to how polemical relations were structured. These analyses serve, as we will see, to intervene within polemical situations.

We identified *tests* or testing as a third mode of judgment. Our conception of a test developed from multiple discussions about Foucault's condensed comments in his lecture series in 1981–82, in which he identified testing as a form of *askēsis*:

> There are I think a number of particular features that characterize the test and distinguish it from abstinence. First, the test always includes a certain questioning of the self by the self. Unlike abstinence, a test basically involves knowing what you are capable of, whether you can do a particular kind of thing and see it through. You may succeed or fail, win or lose in a test, and through this kind of open game of the test it is a matter of locating, of measuring how far you have advanced of knowing basically where you are and what you are. There is an aspect of self-knowledge in the test, which does not exist in the simple application of abstinence. Second, the test should always be accompanied by a certain work of thought on itself.[18]

It seemed to us that tests were operating at multiple orders of observation: for those asking themselves how they might enter such situations, and not only to abstain oneself from the complex field of polemic; for those seeking to stay close to and observe but not get trapped in the terms of polemic; and for those who have found the discursive possibilities of the first two positions so entrapping that the only question is how to leave, to find another position from which to speak, as well as the question of what one can say from that position and to whom.

Rather than follow these conceptual orientations toward inquiry into instances—for example, interviewing writers and editors at *Charlie Hebdo*—actors and others associated with the film *Innocence of Muslims*, and anthropologists who have previously written on blasphemy, insult, religion, and media, we decided to identify a different work site, one that could put the instances, concepts, and questions we had gathered into a longer time frame and a deeper set of case materials.

In mid-September 2012 Rushdie published *Joseph Anton*, his third-person account of the experience of writing *The Satanic Verses* and of the ten years in hiding after the declaration of the fatwa. The name *Joseph Anton* was the pseudonym under which he would live, a composite of Joseph Conrad and Anton Chekhov. We decided to take up the occasion of its publication to engage with this complex historical event, the Rushdie affair, relative to the questions we had posed in the instances we had been working on.

The Actual: Alert, Trial, Denunciation

The publication in 1999 of Francis Chateauraynaud and Didier Torny's *Les sombres précurseurs: De l'alerte et du risque*, marked a trend in French sociology that developed a pragmatic approach to argument and conflict. Their mode of analysis pays attention to how actors grasp situations pragmatically and how alerts and criticisms are taken seriously enough to transform norms/institutions; they focus on the procedures that are available within dispute situations, as well as the temporal transformations and modifications. How does a situation become an affair? What are the characteristics of such situations? In their text, the two sociologists develop a typology (*figures*) of seven configurations or "regimes of test" (*régime d'épreuve*) of the constraints through which an affair is produced: vigilance, alert, controversy, trial, crisis, polemic, normalization:

> Each of these figures provides support for or forms of expression of different kinds of actors. The identification of how to pass from one configuration or testing regime to another can be made from a set of features or parameters.[19]

This grid of parameters was extremely useful in making visible the steps through which a series of transformations took place, before the Rushdie event was structured (a) as a polemic and (b) as turning on the denunciation of Rushdie as a blasphemer and (c) on self-justification through claims to the political right of freedom of speech.

A selection of parameters and configurations turned out to be perspicacious as a lens through which to take up the corpus of approximately one hundred texts and documents that our Labinar group had assembled.

The Rushdie archive we compiled was organized chronologically by year (1988–2012), distinguished by genre (news articles, serious speech acts by protagonists in the unfolding affair highlighting their changing positions, academic interventions in and observations about the affair) and tagged by terms that we had found of interest whilst working initially on instances (self-positioning; form of justification; mode of judgment).

Five parameters organizing three configurations, from Chateauraynaud and Torny, proved to be particularly illuminating for understanding how a

Table 2 Configurations

	Alert	Trial	Polemic
Agent	Whistleblower	Plaintiff	Denouncer
Dominant activity	Demands action, or verification	Accusation/ Imputation of responsibility	Confrontation of principles of judgment
Temporal modality	Orientation toward the future, reversibility, duration with variable geometry (or topology)	Orientation toward the past; Irreversibility; Long duration	Logic of rebound and of permanent revelation
Regulatory instance	Message toward a power of action	Complaint toward an instance of judgment	Medias
Mode of existence of victims	Potential victim (s)	Identified victim(s)	Exhibition
Interpretive work	Interpretation of the state of things	Interpretation of the intentions of people	Interpretation of underlying ideologies
Dominant proof/ evidence	Salience, detachable discontinuity	Investigation, pièces à convictions	Rhetoric
Support from others	Decisive role of experts and administrators	Predominance of witnesses	Strong presence of intellectuals
Production	Monitoring tools, tools for control and risk management	Jurisprudence	Collective representation
Prototype	Alerte à la côté de boeuf	Contaminated blood affair	Heidelberg Appeal
Limit figure	Prophecy of doom	Paranoia	Defamation

series of episodes were transformed into an affair between September 1988 and February 1989. The three configurations were as follows: alert, trial, and polemic. The parameters were the following: dominant activity, temporal modality, regulatory instance, mode of existence of victims, and interpretive work (see table 2).

September 1988: Alert

As Rushdie reports in *Joseph Anton,* on the day he received the bound proofs of *The Satanic Verses,* Rushdie was visited by a person whom he considered to be a friend, the journalist Madhu Jain of *India Today.* She was visiting the UK on holiday, and on meeting Rushdie, and having seen he was in possession of the proof, asked to read the book. He conceded to the request. After having read it, she asked to interview him and to publish an excerpt in the paper. Nine days before the book was published, the paper ran the review and interview under the headline: "An Unequivocal Attack on Religious

Fundamentalism."[20] The last sentence of the piece stated that the novel was "bound to trigger an avalanche of protests."[21]

Given that a small but vocal voice of agitation against the book had already started, the review catalyzed and ramified events. The review functioned as the first major amplifier of protest. Although Rushdie concedes in his memoir that with hindsight and rereading the review, the review itself was evenhanded, ultimately it was bookended by the only statements to which anyone would pay attention. Furthermore, the review broke their friendship, since regardless of her intention the effect of the review was, for Rushdie, to betray both the work (of creation) and the life (of the creator).

With respect to the heuristic parameters made available by Chateauraynaud and Torny, Jain's self-positioning is that of an interpreter of state of affairs that call for "alert," as opposed to an interpretation of Rushdie's intentions or of any underlying ideology. Furthermore, a future temporal orientation prevails in her short review, in which victims exist in potential.

The only other person in India to have read an advance copy, Khushwant Singh, an Indian novelist and journalist, proposed a ban on the book in the interest of public safety. Singh was at the time an editorial advisor for the newly established office of Penguin in India. He recommended without hesitation that Penguin not publish an Indian edition. Singh's two core concerns were what he considered to be Rushdie's undermining of the status of Prophet Mohammad's divine revelation in the novel and the portrayal of a brothel in which women took the names of Mohammad's wives; "it was sheer bad taste."[22] Singh thus mobilizes the regulatory instance of the configuration of alert—the demand of a preventative action to avoid catastrophe.

The confluence of these two tropes, "the novel is an attack on Islam" and "it is necessary to protect publics from publics' reactions" were crystalized in the use made of the statements of Jain and Singh, by conservative Indian politicians, particularly Syed Shahabuddin, whose open letter to Rushdie was titled "You Did This with Satanic Forethought, Mr. Rusdhie."[23] Shahabuddin's letter was an important amplifier of the coding of Rushdie's text as *insult*, combining it with a legal framing.

Shahabuddin's intervention was one among a number of efforts, including efforts in the UK, to transform a configuration of *alert* into one of *trial*:

> Here in India our laws are very clear. Though ignorance of law is no excuse, let me instruct you so that you are more careful if you wish to sell in India. Article 295A of the Indian Penal Code says: Whoever, with deliberate and malicious intent of outraging the religious feelings of any class of citizens of

India, by words either spoken or written, . . . or otherwise insults or attempts to insult the religion or the religious beliefs of that class, shall be punished with imprisonment or with fine.[24]

His letter was published on October 13, 1988, and a week later India banned the book. The ban came from the Finance Ministry, under Section 11 of the Customs Act, which prevented the UK edition from being imported. The ministry stated that the ban "did not detract from the literary and artistic merit" of his work. As such, this was the first of many failed attempts to transform the situation into a juridical scene.

In this first episode, we have a situation in which two people alerted a public, in this case the readers of *India Today*, the publishing house and then the government of the *potential* victims of the text. A legal framing was offered but ultimately was not activated, and potential victims were rendered as actual victims. Shahabuddin went on to write:

> As patriots and nationalists we should not only be glad but grateful to the government for its sensitivity to the anguish felt by an important sector of our people at this deliberate offense to their religious feelings, for its readiness to share their sense of injury and to express its concern in the administrative idiom.

In addition to this being an administrative idiom, the novel itself, crucially, was not, at this point (October 1988), publicly denounced as blasphemous. Following the schema of alert, a message was rather sent toward a specific agent capable of action, which at this moment was the Indian Ministry of Finance.

November 1988: Toward Denunciation

Two weeks after the ban in India, in November 1988, Rushdie returned from the Booker Prize Award Ceremony in London, at which *The Satanic Verses* did not win. He found a voicemail message waiting for him. He had been due to travel to Johannesburg four days later to deliver a keynote lecture at a conference on apartheid and censorship, at the invitation of the anti-apartheid paper, *Weekly Mail*. The invitation had the backing of the African National Congress. The voice delivering the message simply stated, "I must speak to you before you fly."[25]

As Rushdie recounts the episode, he was in a strange mood. He had wished that a Booker win could have brought back the "quality defense" for his book, amid growing public argument, alerts, and the ban in India. He was told straightforwardly by the person on the end of the line that for his own safety and the good of the movement against apartheid, he should not travel to South Africa. His presence, he was told, would split the Congress of South African Writers.

The Muslim quorum had threated to resign en masse should he travel to the city and the congress of writers could not risk the consequences of such a split. The Muslim South African writer Fatima Meer had stated, "in the final analysis it is the Third World that Rushdie attacks."[26] The insult/attack coding was growing and victims were being added.

The week in which his invitation had been revoked due to the mounting pressure from within the writers congress, the government of South Africa banned the novel, claiming that the novel was "disgusting not only to Muslims, but to any reader who holds clear values of decency and culture."[27] Whereas the Indian government had explicitly not taken up the text itself as an object of denunciation, the ban in South Africa is the first moment when an authority that had the capacity to use sanctions offered reasoning about the worth of the text itself.

Toward Blasphemy: Institutional Arrangements and a Discursive Field

As in judiciary practice, polemics allows for no possibility of an equal discussion: it examines a case; it isn't dealing with an interlocutor, it is processing a suspect; it collects the proofs of his guilt, designates the infraction he has committed, and pronounces the verdict and sentences him. In any case, what we have here is not on the order of a shared investigation; the polemicist tells the truth in the form of his judgment and by virtue of the authority he has conferred on himself.

—Michel Foucault[28]

A UK Action Committee on Islamic Affairs (UKACIA) was established on 11 October 1988 to coordinate protests and other activities regarding *The Satanic Verses*. It began when the Islamic Foundation of Leicester was alerted of the blasphemous contents of the book by Jamaat-e-Islami Hind a Sunni Islamic organization in India, connected to the Pakistani Islamist party Jamaat-e-Islami. It is important to note that throughout October and November, whilst there were judgments from Muslims as to the blasphemous character of the text, the act of public denunciation had not yet been able to be produced.

Jeanne Favret-Saada, in her essay "Rushdie et compagnie: Préalables à une anthropologie du blasphème" makes explicit that historians and others

"I propose therefore the existence of a jurisdictional apparatus (in a broad sense of the term) composed of four instances:

1   An institutional arrangement (*montage institutionnel* [MI]), reservoir of potential 'theological' interpretations and potential public sanctions.
2   A denouncer [X], relying on a 'theological' competence to demand sanctions.
3   A "blasphemer" [Y], the accused, whose statement 'God is not' is considered degrading for 'God.'
4   Finally, an authority [Z], capable of imposing sanctions.

[1]

The formula for any communication concerning a "blasphemy" becomes:
[X] to Z by virtue of [MI]: [Y] said: 'God is not . . .' "[2]

[1]Jeanne Favret-Saada, "Rushdie et compagnie"; "Je pose donc l'existence d'un dispositif judiciaire (au sens large du terme) comportant quatre instances:1. un montage institutionnel [MI], réservoir d'interprétations 'théologiques' virtuelles et de sanctions publiques virtuelles - montage qui préexiste aux acteurs, dans lequel ils sont pris, et dont ils ont une connaissance relative. 2. Un dénonciateur [X], se fondant sur une compétence 'théologique' pour exiger des sanctions ; 3. Un 'blasphémateur' [Y], l'accusé, dont l'énoncé 'Dieu' est n'est considéré comme dégradant pour 'Dieu'; 4. Enfin, une autorité [Z], susceptible de prendre des sanctions."

[2]Ibid., "La formule de toute communication à propos d'un 'blasphème' devient alors: [X] à Z, en vertu de [MI] : [Y] a dit: 'Dieu est n.' "

have misidentified the object of an accusation of blasphemy.[29] Her orientation to an anthropology of blasphemy identifies a tripartite relation established in a blasphemy accusation, which only subsequently can encompass the referent, in this case Rushdie's text. The blasphemy accusation, in other words, is not generated by and does not rely on any particular content. An accusation, rather, is the outcome of institutional support to make discursive acts sayable, hearable, and capable of being sustained.

She develops an interpretive model for understanding the accusation of blasphemy from the logic of the practice of witchcraft accusations in the Bocage, Western France, published as *Les Mots, Les Morts, Les Sorts* (1977).[30] In her model of blasphemy, the starting node is a denouncer demanding sanctions. The denouncer denounces something or someone to an authority capable of producing sanctions. The denouncer-authority relation must be supported by an institutional arrangement, venues, which are capable of making theological claims as well as a range of possible public sanctions. The denunciation of the novel and the novelist as blasphemous is thus interpreted as an effect of a system of serious speech acts, rather than the content per se being a cause of such a denunciation.

By October 21, 1988, UKACIA had several hundred thousand signatories to a petition protesting the publication and calling on the publisher Viking Penguin for the book's withdrawal. In their own narrative, when the appeal was ignored the action committee redoubled their efforts writing to all Muslim ambassadors in London calling for a ban on the book. The Iranian *charge d'affaires* Akhondzadeh Basti, is reported to have forwarded it to Tehran.

To rewrite the episodes in terms of Favret-Saada's model: a series of denouncer-authority relations was established before the institutional conditions could be created to make the accusation of blasphemy. These conditions went through a stage of alerts, a failed effort to mobilize legal framings and then a successful polemical framing in which a blasphemy accusation was made possible:

1   Jamaat-e-Islami Hind, a Muslim political organization in India, did not pursue the accusation of blasphemy within India. Arguably the institutional arrangement for a framing of insult/administration resolution overrode any attempts to create conditions for an accusation of blasphemy to be heard. Shahubbudin's legal framing was not mobilized.

2   Jamaat-e-Islami Hind contacted the Islamic Foundation of Leicester, among other actors in the UK, to alert them of the blasphemy originating in their country. The call was echoed by the Grand Sheikh of Al-Azhar University in Cairo, Gad el-Haq Ali Gad el-Haq.[31]

3   Institutional arrangements were created when the Saudi government funded and coordinated the UK Action Committee.

4   The UK Action Committee unsuccessfully attempted to have the author tried under the UK blasphemous libel law (a process which took several years— the law was repealed in 2008), as well as to have the book banned under the Public Order Act (1986) and the Race Relations Act (1976).

5   After an unsuccessful attempt to stage a book burning in Bolton on December 2, 1988, the Action Committee was more successful in January 1989, garnering widespread media attention for the same genre of event in Bradford. With the transition from legal complaint to media event, we have the first characteristic of the establishment of a scene of polemic.

6   The UK Action Committee claimed to have then alerted the Iranian *charge d'affaires* at the time of the book burning.[32] An authority, the ayatollah, is at this point finally willing to draw on an institutional arrangement with *sufficient*—but not exclusive—theological authority, and willing to name a form of sanction appropriate to the form of the accusation: "Khomeini as *mujtahid* was a qualified fatwa giver and his verdict to have Rushdie killed, passed on February 14, 1989, has to be seen as a response to the initiative of *istifta* (i.e., he was asked for a fatwa)."[33]

7   A situation of polemic was entrenched with the establishment of the International Committee for the Defense of Salman Rushdie and His Publishers,
an organization of intellectuals which sought among other things to repeal
the UK's blasphemy law. The committee's rationale was that a free society
should have no limits on the freedom of expression.[34]

Actual Discordancy, or, the Illegitimacy of Indetermination: Asad's Rushdie

But it is the political model that is the most powerful today. Polemics defines
alliances, recruits partisans, unites interests or opinions, represents a party; it establishes the other as an enemy, an upholder of opposed interests against which
one must fight until the moment this enemy is defeated and either surrenders or
disappears.

—Michel Foucault[35]

Talal Asad published two articles in 1990 on the Rushdie affair, reproduced
in his book *Genealogies of Religion* (1993). They appear as the fourth and final part of the book under the heading "Polemics." He writes in the second
of the two essays, "Ethnography, Literature, and Politics: Some Readings
and Uses of Salman Rushdie's *The Satanic Verses*" (published when he had
taken a position at the New School for Social Research, after having left
Hull, in the UK):

my aim is to intervene in the political debate surrounding the publication
of the book by raising some questions about the ambiguous heritage of liberalism as it affects non-Western immigrants in the modern European state,
particularly in Britain.

There is, within this aim, a claim to knowledge about the experience of
immigrants in the modern European state, and in this case the non-
Western immigrant population at stake is Muslim. The position from which
he writes matters since as he states, "We are all already constituted subjects, placed in networks of power."[36]
    Asad aims to pose questions which Rushdie refused: about the actuality
of the experience of immigrants in Britain. Asad's critique of Rushdie centers
on a diagnosis that Rushdie's problem, his object and objective—to think
through and to write a (funny, vicious, sardonic) novel about the relation

of faith in divine revelation, to the shifting cultural politics of living which undergird and are inflected by faith in absolute truth—is not recognizable as a problem to "most Muslims."[37] He has, in other words, a different diagnosis of the problem of modernity and of the nefarious origins of Rushdie's indetermination—of what a modern attitude to religiosity might be within the ambiguous heritage of liberalism.

In our view, Asad's project investigates and argues for the legitimacy of the countermodern.[38] He seeks to critique Rushdie's exemplification of the modern ethos, by way of a *tragic* narration of forms of life increasingly constituted by—and partially resisting—the technological projects of Western secular modernity. He proposes to grasp the historicity of the West, to understand genealogically the anthropological project of describing Others in relation to the "mobile powers" of the technological projects of modernization.

The article takes "Enlightenment discourses" as its starting point for a critique of such projects, discourses that "inscribe on the world a unity in its own image."[39] Two familiar steps are quickly made: the first is to situate anthropological knowledge within this characterization of "Enlightenment discourses" and then to inscribe anthropology, and ethnographic representation in particular, within the legacy of imperialism.[40]

The case of Rushdie is taken as an example of how such "imperializing power has made itself felt in and through many other kinds of writing not least the kind we call 'fiction.' "[41] Such an imperializing power turns on the capacity to produce descriptions and thus Asad's critical strategy is to demonstrate the manner in which Rushdie's novel is actually a description of Islam from within the presuppositions and historical conditions of the "West."

Asad quotes two contradictory readings of the novel by Rushdie, specifically on the question of whether the novel is "about" the history of Islam. In his open letter to the prime minister of India in September 1988, in response to the banning of the book, Rushdie is quoted as writing, "Let's remember that the book in question isn't actually about Islam," stressing that the section of the book which was taken to have caused offense (part 2, titled "Mahound"), in which a prophet living in a city made of sand (which keeps dissolving), receives a revelation, occurs within a dream sequence. Rushdie exclaims, "How much further from history could one get?"[42] Six months later, in March 1989, once alert had been rendered as polemic, he was denounced and was living under the sign of religious judgment, calling for his death. Asad quotes Rushdie from the *New York Review of Books*:

A powerful tribe of clerics has taken over Islam. One may not discuss Muhammad as if he were human, with human virtues and weaknesses. One may not
discuss the growth of Islam as a historical phenomenon. . . . Inside my novel,
its characters seek to become fully human by facing up to the great facts of
love, death, and (with or without God) the life of the soul. Outside it, the
forces of inhumanity are on the march. . . . Now that the battle has spread to
Britain, I only hope it will not be lost by default. It is time for us to choose.[43]

"Why the contradictory readings?" asks Asad. The real political intention for
writing the novel is unmasked in the second quotation. This second quotation, in Asad's view, undermines both Rushdie's and other commentators'
judgments that the novel was not a (polemical) representation of religion,
but an exploration of faith and doubt.[44] "Representation of religious doubt"
in Asad's unveiling is "a rhetorical tactic" since Rushdie "has often told us
that he lost his faith in religion a long time ago." Furthermore, Rushdie is
revealed as equating Islam *tout court* with "forces of inhumanity."

Neither point is quite true. As Rushdie recounts in *Joseph Anton*, Rushdie
never "had" faith. He was raised culturally as a Muslim, by a father who
engaged seriously with the Qur'an as a historical artifact of a divine revelation, the veracity of which (the revelation) his father did not doubt. Rather,
doubt, in his father's eyes, entered at the level of writing, reproduction, and
transmission of divine revelation.[45] Furthermore, the Manichaean speech
act, "It's time for us to choose," is an agonistic speech act within a situation
which has been worked over as polemical, rather than polemic being the
starting point from which the novel is written.

Asad selects a quotation from one of Rushdie's many exercises in self-
justification to illustrate Rushdie's modernity and juxtaposes it with countermodern forms of life. He has Rushdie recount the story of Aadam Aziz,
the patriarch in *Midnight's Children*, and finds within Rushdie's narrative a
core problem of modernity. Aziz

loses his faith and is left with "a hole inside him, a vacancy in a vital inner chamber." I too, possess the same God-shaped hole. Unable to accept
the unarguable absolutes of religion, I have tried to fill up the hole with
literature.[46]

Asad mobilizes a critique, associated with Edward Said who later dissoci-
ated himself from its vulgar rendition, of the function of literature as a pedagogy of bourgeois sensibility.

Asad exposes what he claims are two core assumptions of modernity as an ethos: (a) "the assumption that the discourse called Literature can fill the role previously performed by religious textuality" and (b) "the remarkable value given to self-fashioning." The latter (self-fashioning) can be identified by Asad as being recognizable to "Western middleclass readers of 'literary' novels but not to most Muslims in Britain or the Indian subcontinent."[47] The former claim requires reading the text as a successful effort at salvation, making whole, or else its tragic narration as an impossible task. Either way, Asad misses the core point articulated by Foucault, and arguably attempted to be instantiated by Rushdie, that the modern ethos is characterized by the *problematization* of the self as an autonomous subject and the pathos of a limit attitude to itself and its reality.

In Asad's hermeneutics of suspicion, "doubt" in Rushdie's work "is neither the beginning nor the end of an exploration into new forms of moral and political existence."[48] On the contrary, Rushdie is read as articulating a determined position—"personal prejudice against Islam"[49]—secured in advance which knowingly had the effect of insult. The claim characterizes *The Satanic Verses* as a polemical work, rather than polemic being the outcome of several months of what Favret-Saada refers to as *montage institutionnel*. Five years of work, we should therefore surmise from Asad's reading, were in order for Rushdie to write a thinly veiled and insulting representation of Islam, from a position which he had already secured, that of the atheist, bourgeois, modern.

We observe that Asad's reading is not the only one and in fact was part of the *montage institutionnel* and discursive practices which sustained the affair as polemic. Anthropologically, we ask how writing the book, and writing (and living) through numerous responses to the book, constituted ongoing testing for Rushdie regarding what he had been doing, as well as how the affair constitutes a test for an anthropologist of the contemporary, interested in both Rushdie and what his observers thought they were doing with their observations.

The events surrounding Rushdie, his own and others' speech acts about the affair can be seen as having turned on claims about the distance or proximity between truth and conduct. In the effort to bring together truth and conduct, one risks self-justification and self-deception. To the degree that this effort breaks down, the degree that one can make visible and sayable how it broke down, and the afterlife of that breakdown and effort at repair, we take up the action with a mood of pathos.

For commentators, such as Asad, to articulate a problem of truth and conduct under conditions of modernity is to unwittingly reproduce the terms of secular modernity as an imperial project. His intervention was narrated tragically through the identification of the power relations at play within "the West" between secular liberal moderns and their Others. Asad wrote that the

"major ideas [anthropology] uses to grasp its subjects (non-modern, local traditional) are often dependent on its contrastive sense of the modern."[50]

Asad reproduces the terms of this contrast by highlighting, in order to evaluate, the function of modernity as a metric for forms of life.

As anthropologists of the contemporary we situate Asad's efforts as a constituent part of the configurations of the actual. Our efforts operate and take up a different problem than Asad's does. We have identified more specific parameters and metrics for tracking the moving ratios of modernity; ratios of practice that move to the degree that they are temporal as well as historical; ratios of practices that are modern to the degree that they can be characterized by their breakdowns, as well as efforts through vocational practice to repair such breakdowns.

To take up breakdowns as irrevocable and only as loss is tragic and countermodern. To disregard loss is comic to the degree that temporary resolutions are narrated and ironic to the degree that loss is ignored. In Michael Fischer and Mehdi Abedi's 1990 essay "Bombay Talkies, the Word and the World: Salman Rushdie's *Satanic Verses*," the authors provide a detailed, scholarly, and witty reading of both *The Satanic Verses* as a novel and the social context in which reactions to the novel were generated. A space of complex comedic possibilities are claimed to have been opened, between text and context, through the "critical functions" of the novel:

Such postmodern literature attempts to reconnect in Gestalt-switching ways the ruins of the past, contemporary politics and technologies, and the emergent interreligious, intercommunal interideological world of cultural inter-férences (interreferences, interferences).[51]

As we understand it, the tragic, comic, and ironic moods miss the problematic ratio of breakdown and repair.

Vindication and Pathos

Aiming at vindication—but running the danger of self-justification—the narrative mood of Rushdie's memoir, *Joseph Anton*, is comedic; all's well that ends well, for now. The book is a third-person account of Rushdie as Joseph Anton, the pseudonym under which he lived guarded by the Special Branch (Security Service) of the London Metropolitan Police Force.

On the December 24, 1990, Rushdie, after almost two years under police protection, and frustrated with the stasis and stultification of the situation, accepted a possible means of undoing the fatwa and repairing his relationship with British Muslims and by extension with Islam. We see in this episode a marker of the pathos of the affair. Through this episode we seek to refuse both the tragic and the comedic, to articulate a different afterlife and significance for the affair.

An Egyptian dental surgeon with a private practice in London's exclusive Harley Street, Hesham el-Essawy, had taken it upon himself to attempt to mediate between Rushdie and a group of six Islamic scholars from assorted Muslim organizations, who were for the most part Egyptians living in London. Everyone agreed that the affair had been a "tragic misunderstanding."

Essawy et alia wanted to reclaim Rushdie, as a member of the Muslim intelligentsia; Rushdie wanted to be reclaimed. Essawy told him that "all that was needed was a gesture of goodwill."[52] This gesture, he was told, was simple: what Rushdie was asked to show was sincerity in his efforts to repair the damage caused by this tragic misunderstanding and this could only be done by *shahada*, an honest recitation that there is no God but God and Muhammad is his Prophet.

Four days later Rushdie published a piece in the *Times* of London, "Why I Have Embraced Islam":

"I have been finding my own way," he wrote, "towards an intellectual understanding of religion, and religion for me has always meant Islam. . . . I am certainly not a good Muslim, but I am able to say that I am a Muslim; in fact it is a source of happiness to say that I am now inside, and a part of, the community whose *values* have always been close to my heart. I have in the past described the furore over *The Satanic Verses* as a family quarrel. Well, I'm now inside the family and now Muslims can talk to Muslims and continue the process of reconciliation that began with my Christmas Eve meeting with six Muslim scholars. The meeting, which was described in some sections of the press as a defeat, was in fact a victory for compassion, understanding and tolerance."[53]

Rushdie agreed at his Christmas Eve meeting to desist from seeking a paperback edition of *The Satanic Verses* and any further translations. His acceptance of this condition was denounced in the press by Francis Bennion,

an academic and lawyer who had been part of the International Rushdie
Defense Committee. The committee had been established through the collaboration of Article 19, the then recently established (1987) London-based
human rights organization whose mandate is the defense and promotion
of freedom of expression with American PEN, a literary and human rights
organization working to safeguard and promote literature and literary fel-
lowship. Rushdie was, for Bennion, no longer worth defending.[54]

One of Rushdie's vocal advocates, who continued to support him, was
British feminist novelist Fay Weldon. Weldon's pamphlet *Sacred Cows*, published in July of 1989, was a defense of Rushdie, an attack on the antilib-
eral values of fundamentalist Islam, and a muddled list of freely associated
problems with British society, of which the affair was claimed as symptomatic. Rushdie's cause and character was being mobilized and inserted
into two sets of values: the liberal-secular and the Islamic, by himself and
others.

Rushdie's effort to navigate available positions and to reconcile himself
with himself was a spectacular failure, both externally and internally. The
judgment from Iran remained as did his judgment of himself. In a diary
entry on New Year's Day 1991, Rushdie wrote the following of the motion
which he had instituted, contributed to, participated in, affected, and had
in turn been affected by:

> Ever since I made my compromise with the Muslim scholars on Christmas
> Eve, I have been feeling sick; sick at heart and in my stomach. This isn't me,
> it isn't me. One of the mullahs I spoke with is on TV, vilifying homosexuals.
> One of the scholars I met with has written an article saying it is ok to slap your
> wife if she is disobedient. What have I done indeed. I repeat my reasons over
> and over. I wanted ordinary Muslims to know I wasn't their enemy. I wanted
> to argue the need for a better, more open, less repressive Muslim society and I
> thought I could do it better from inside the room. It all sounds like nonsense.
> Like self-justification. This is the worst moment of my life.[55]

A space of values, of subscribing to values of defending values, had replaced
the search for forms through which to encounter indeterminations in ideas
and ratios of truth and conduct. The indetermination of the novel, how to
write about the historicity of revelation when available cultural forms have
broken down, was replaced with the assurance of those participating in the
affair, that available values could answer such indetermination.

Rushdie narrates the episode and fallout of his meeting with the Islamic
scholars and cultural leaders, as one of a judgment of himself:

In the afternoon he was taken to a press conference and tried to sound positive. There were interviews for radio and television, with Essawy and without
him. He did not remember what he said. He knew what he was saying to himself. You are a liar, he was saying. You are a liar and a coward and a fool. . . .
He had survived this long because he could put his hand on his heart and
defend every word he had written or said. He had written seriously and with
integrity and everything he said about that had been the truth. Now he had
torn his tongue out of his own mouth, had denied the ability to use the language and ideas that were natural to him. Until this moment he had been
accused of a crime against the belief of others. Now he accused himself, and
found himself guilty, of having committed a crime against himself.[56]

The moving ratio between Rushdie and *Anton,* or rather, Rushdie's distance
and proximity to the *bios* that was *Anton* underscores the pathos of the affair and constitutes a contemporary site of testing. The distance introduced
between Rushdie and Anton was a form to provide motion between a judgment—"you are a liar," Rushdie says to Anton—and vindication of Rushdie
as author of *Joseph Anton.* He had exercised a judgment of himself, and narratively prepared a move toward vindication:

> He had perplexed all his friends and had obliged himself to stand smiling
> alongside those who had vilified him and threatened others, people who had
> acquiesced in the threat of murder made by Iran.[57]

Rushdie, as Anton, had put himself in a serious bind: How could he take
possession of himself and his time under these conditions? His effort at
vindication consisted in martyrdom: he would die for but not kill for ideas.
His judgment of himself as a coward and a liar prompted a new resolve:

> He was learning that to win a fight like this, it was not enough to know what
> one was fighting against. That was easy. He was fighting against the view that
> people could be killed for their ideas, and against the ability of any religion
> to place a limiting point on thought. But he needed, now, to be clear of what
> he was fighting for. Freedom of speech, freedom of the imagination, freedom
> from fear, and the beautiful, ancient art of which he was privileged to be a
> practitioner. Also skepticism, irreverence, doubt, satire, comedy, and unholy
> glee. He would never again flinch from the defense of these things. He had
> asked himself the question: As you are fighting a battle that may cost you your
> life, is the thing for which you are fighting worth losing your life for? And he
> had found it possible to answer: yes.[58]

In 1989, the contrarian Christopher Hitchens, in the *London Review of Books*, argued for the urgency and significance of the events surrounding Rushdie—a coordinated transnational campaign to impose a death sentence on a writer—and for the generality of the appropriate response to this "alarming singularity," to use Hitchens' phrase, that there is nothing particularly "Western" about the felt obligation to defend a fellow writer from such a threat.[59] Further, it goes without saying, defending any person, not just a writer, from such a threat is a contemporary challenge that all traditions must find a form for, if they are to remain more than vehicles for self-justification.

FIVE

Gerhard Richter's Pathos

That the world, through the bios, became that experience through which we know ourselves, that exercise through which we reveal ourselves to ourselves, that exercise through which we transform ourselves or we know ourselves, I think that this is a transformation, an important mutation from the classical Greek thought, in which the bios was the object of a technē, that is to say a reasonable and rational art.

—Michel Foucault[1]

It is very hard for a German not to be tragic. It is equally hard for a German not to fall back upon a sulky irony if the tragic is beyond one's skills or the genre in which one labors. One of Gerhard Richter's most distinctive achievements, one apparently not schematized by the ever-growing number of scholars treating his work and his life, at the deepest level his *manner* of painting—with its pale assonances with his life—is Richter's pathos.

Although *pathos* is an old term, appearing for example in Aristotle's rhetoric, and although it has had a long and varied history, in modernity it finds its places in the realms of theater and medicine.[2] The dictionary definitions of pathos equate it with a form of emotion. In our understanding, this equation is not only incorrect but misleading. *Pathos* is an affect term; it is a structured milieu in which emotions and representations qualify and are shaped within specific forms. Affect is not an emotion in that it is a relational state and not an interior one; affect does not emanate from the subject as the sentimental novels and literature of the eighteenth-century represented emotion.[3]

This relational structure of affect is one reason that the theater was a privileged site of experimentation and experience for a long time. The pathos of pathology in medicine takes place in the doctor-patient scene in which bodily materiality, suffering, and attempts to understand and compensate for disease, suffering, and finitude take their place.[4]

Of course, there are many different kinds of affect; they can be given many different forms. As explained earlier, we have differentiated four moods (pathos, tragedy, irony, and comedy). Gerhard Richter's work, we argue, is cast distinctively and pervasively in a mood of pathos. Furthermore, to complicate the narrative one more turn, while it is certainly contestable that Richter's work could be narrated otherwise than in the form we are giving it, on a second-order level of experience, experimentation, and narrative, we ourselves are self-consciously organizing the material under consideration in a mood of pathos. It follows that the relation of our narrative mood and other interpretations of Richter, by critics or the artist himself, might well be ironic, comic, or in a mood of pathos—so be it.

The manner in which we are taking up Richter's work is what we intend as a contemporary one. The pathos we observe and inscribe follows in the light of Foucault's claim (and its terms) given above as the epigram. Foucault's claim is that the test of *bios* is neither a direct representation of what is nor a straightforward construction of what is. Rather, the problem and the challenge is given a mood of pathos, how to proceed so as to make one's practice an exercise, an experiment, and a test.

In order to make a plausible demonstration of this claim we will have to examine the themes of *technē*, of mood, of mode of subjectivation, and of Richter's paintings' capacity to make visible a *Bild* with a reality effect. Such reality effects make no claim, visually or otherwise, to be totalizing, symbolic, synecdochic, or analogical world pictures. Nor are they a continuation of the unstable relation of painter and subject under the regime of sovereignty. Yet, Richter's overall oeuvre, if not every instance, does carry forward that problem if not the solution. Here is an example, among others, of *Nachleben* and of *Pathosformel*.

I. Technology and *Technē* (1): Interferences

The challenge is as follows: how can what is given as the object of knowledge (savoir) connected to the mastery of technē, at the same time be the site where the truth of the subject we are appears, or is experienced and fulfilled with difficulty? How can the world which is given as the object of knowledge (connaissance) on the basis of the mastery of technē, at the same time be the site where the 'self' is tested as the ethical subject of truth.

—Michel Foucault[5]

Hubertus Butin, curator of a major exhibit of Richter's *Editions* in Berlin in 2011, in his video presentation on the Richter website (and in his published writings) poses the following question as being at the heart of Richter's work: What is an image today?[6]

It is a commonplace to assert that the image currently finds itself in a troubled location between the history of images (art, photography, etc.) and the current global saturation of omnipresent media obtainable at an unprecedented scale and scope. Butin describes Richter as incessantly testing multiple possibilities in order to discover passages through this media-saturated topology, as well as the spectral historical archive.

This characterization can serve as a crisp identification as well as diagnosis of a contemporary problem space. In order to achieve and maintain a contemporary mood, the artist and critics as well as observers must acknowledge the dynamics of this mutually interfering and enhancing activity and attempt to find a form of addressing it by taking it up as an experience, a milieu, a technical challenge, and a test.

Translated into our terms, an initial formulation of the problem space highlights the problem of the presence of *Nachleben* in a modern space, and what to make of them in terms of form and significance. In that light, the working and reworking, accepting and rejecting, with multiple possible forms constitutes the realm of the *Pathosformel*. Finally, as we shall see, in order to complete the series of the parameters of the contemporary, we identify a distinguishing *kairos* for Gerhard Richter that occasions much of his image making in direct, as well as oblique, ways.

From the Technical to *Technē*: *Moiré*

Following established critical conventions, Butin argues that Richter's highly diverse artistic output has been consistently mediated by the use of a range of industrial techniques. Fundamentally, Richter establishes transactions with the world of images by acknowledging the centrality of industrial technique in their production, reproduction, and dissemination. In that sense, Richter has affirmed, albeit with a bittersweet tone, Marcel Duchamp's famous claim that painting was over but that one needed nonetheless to continue making art. In Richter's case, he has restively pursued a practice of painting that is neither nostalgic nor avant-garde. Indeed, how to find a mean, if that is what it is, constitutes an ongoing challenge for him. Experimenting, checking, and evaluating the forms he restlessly produces organize, we argue, a test not only for the daily practice of the artist but for critics and observers as well.

Throughout his career, Richter has been resolutely antimodernist, if by that one understands the modernist commitment to consist in the motivation to show the inherent worth of rendering painting as nothing but painting through finding means to show that the materials and their arrangement on a canvas refer to themselves and themselves alone. It is not that Richter totally rejects the high modernist striving for abstraction and rupture as historical conditions but only that he takes up abstraction and rupture not as goals in and of themselves but as available techniques and thereby sees his challenge as finding ways to make them function differently. These premises and practices of high modernism in the arts are by now not so much obliterated or irrelevant for Richter but part of a moving ratio with the near future.

As an example of this refunctioning attitude and practice, Butin picks out *moiré*. *Moiré* refers to an error in printing technology when a mistake occurs in the process that produces a blurring or an inconsistency in the image. Richter takes up the effect produced by a technical imperfection, abstracts it from the norms that classify it as an error, and instead lets it stand as a technical procedure that could be used to produce distinctive image effects.

Another example of this opportunistic and transformative approach concerns color. For Richter, gray is the absence of color; hence it is the tone best suited to escape or at least reduce referentiality and meaning.[7] Again, he refuses to take up gray in a high modernist mode in which the purported purity and self-referentiality of the color become its connotation as in Yves Klein's use of blue as both transcendental in and of itself as well as simultaneously the artist's avant-garde signature. Richter is fully aware of Malevich's color squares and their claim to purity as well as the twentieth-century tradition of such monochrome canvasses that followed these early breakthroughs and ruptures, leading, for example, to the work of a painter like Robert Ryman, whose white or nearly white canvasses continue that mode and for whom Richter expresses some admiration. Richter's test has been to acknowledge and accept the place of this tradition and then to interfere with its use of color as an end in itself. Rather, he subsequently strives to formulate and put into practice a response to the challenge of what kind of techniques constitute high modernism, how they can be disaggregated—and how, thereby they become available to redefine the artist's *technē* as a site of production and experience.

Butin illustrates the general points about technique, color, and Richter's "aesthetic of absence" through the example of Richter's famous painting of his daughter Betty, her blond hair and red robe vividly foregrounded. This seemingly realistic portrait has received multiple critical interpretations.

These range from blunt criticism of the painting as sentimental and commercial to a sophisticated interpretation of the figure of Betty, who we see with her head turned away, as really an instantiation of Walter Benjamin's famous evocation of Paul Klee's *Angelus Novus* which Benjamin narrates as looking back toward the storms of history while being blown forward into the future.

Butin, by examining the painting more closely, and no doubt after discussions with Richter, points out that what Betty is portrayed as gazing at is not the history of capitalism, but rather a contrastive gray canvas (whose bottom edge is visible in the painting) in the background. By so doing, Richter establishes a relationship between the photorealism of the dominant figure in the foreground and the gray tableau with its presumed lack of meaning or referentiality in the background. Such an internal relationship thereby functions as an interference technique disrupting or disqualifying those looking for direct reference and its associated meaning but equally for those asserting the impossibility or definitional absence of reference or meaning.

One could say that Richter wants it both ways by having both figural and nonfigural focal points; or one could see that painting as a particularly provocative and successful exemplar of how an insistence on the presence of *Nachleben* can be combined with an assertive realism (learned techniques from his days in the East German Academy no doubt) to produce a *Pathosformel* in which the necessity and futility of this arrangement presses the artist, critic, and spectator into a domain of visibility (and thought) that qualifies as contemporary.

Another example that Butin discusses is Richter's use of color charts. The artist has experimented with them for many years. One of their attractions for Richter is that color charts do not depict anything; they are simply, as it were, an arrangement of the spectrum of color understood as a fact of nature, produced by techniques that have broken free of trade secrets or artistic genius. In that light, a leading art historian of modernism, Rosalind Krauss, has nominated color charts as "an emblem of modernity" because they only appeared in the early twentieth century as part of the industrialization of paint (again, Duchamp).

One could say that this aspect of modernism is a *Nachleben* in Richter's present but not one he makes actual in the manner that his modernist predecessors have done. Rather, he sees it as an ordinary thing of the world, open to be taken up in a second-order manner by artist or critic. In response to the ordinariness, Richter does not turn to a craft moment of mixing his own paints and making that craft dimension visible but rather he takes the colors charts and rearranges the spectrum. By so doing, the ordering of the industrial paint charts is accepted as an ordinary thing of the world but not its naturalness. The flow through a gradated series from one end of the spectrum to another that one can see in any paint store is taken as a gradated series from what was taken to be one end of the spectrum of visibility for human eyes to the other. In sum, Richter is not taking color to be an industrialized nature; rather, he is taking it as a series of what has been taken to be an industrialized nature so that it can be arranged and rearranged.

What technique does Richter employ in order to render the quality of denaturalized seriality visible? The answer is another technique that clearly fascinates Richter, one he is attracted to and yet, once again, wants to reproblematize—chance. Richter developed a simple technique whereby the serial order could be redistributed; he took the individual color chips, put them in a container, and then arbitrarily picked them out one by one and placed them on the chart. Richter, however, did not leave the implementation of his search for such a technique, as it were, to chance or arbitrariness. Rather, once again, he combined chance with planning—systematizing the variations that he had first discovered by this crude method—thereby undermining the modernist reference to the play of chance in and of itself by accepting the modernist gambit but mediating it by introducing technological ordering practices. By so doing, the arbitrariness was not fetishized but made visible as a practice thereby opening it up to further uses and understandings.

A third type of interference that Butin discusses is that of iconography. Richter has experimented over the years with a series of paintings of candles. Candles were a well-known part of the *vanitas* genre that flourished in the seventeenth century in which the closeness of death and the foolishness of worldly pleasures and distractions were brought into view. It would seem to be unproblematic to connect Richter's paintings of candles (and an occasional skull) to the *vanitas* paintings and critics have, often in a didactic tone.

This pedagogy, however, is misleading. First, Butin points out that several of Richter's paintings are of a single candle which in and of itself violates the traditional iconographic conventions of always including more than one candle. Consequently, Richter's self-conscious transformation of the canon should be understood, once again, as a technique of interference lest the viewer or critic assume that Richter's candles have a fixed meaning carried forward through the ages.

That being said, it probably is true that they do have a referent, the *Nachleben* of the *vanitas* tradition and the specters of the meaning they once had as techniques of moral pedagogy in a world long since gone but not entirely forgotten. It follows that to claim that Richter's choice to depict candles figuratively is entirely arbitrary is unconvincing; if that were the case not only would there have been no reason to depict them, but there would be nothing with which to interfere.

Richter amplifies the iconographical and semantic interference by the different techniques of painting within the image: the candles are painted as mottled and other parts of the canvas are overpainted with strong black splotches. Hence, and while it is true, as Butin claims, that such juxtaposition of seemingly figural and seemingly nonfigural aspects on a single canvas ultimately highlights the materiality of the paint itself, it seems to us that this gesture reaches beyond a modernist gesture priming the visibility and materiality of paint per se, but rather a more complicated interference that retains the candles as survivals or *Nachleben*.

There is a tension here between the ironic and the pathetic. The tension, we hold, may well present a temptation for the critic but not for the artist or the anthropological observer. Why bother undermining or ironizing something long since passed into the past? Why bring it into the frame if not to show that it has an afterlife or survival. If nothing else it is evocative of the presence of death and our current problems with giving it form, meaning, or significance. In a word, Richter's multiple experiments with painting candles can be seen plausibly as experiments in contemporary technique. Such technique is almost certainly not an end in itself but a way of facilitating the recognition of an experience or the lack of a form of something which calls for a *technē*. In a word, the candle paintings might well point to the vanity of certain critics while rendering palpable an affect of the tensions of contemporary experience.

Finally, and most unconvincingly, Butin turns to Richter's 9/11 paintings. He judges these paintings to be successful and moving ones because of their avoidance of direct representation of the plane crashing into one of the twin towers. For Butin, the way in which Richter avoids such realism is through the use of his famous and branded technique, the squeegee. Over the figurative representation of one of the twin towers, Richter deploys his squeegee to scrape and move the paint across the surface of the canvas so as to partially obscure the underlying representation. In that manner, the critic claims the viewer is provided with a distance in order to reflect on the event's meaning and thereby to remain loyal to Richter's oft-pronounced desire to remain free of ideological constraints of any sort.

Here, in our opinion, Richter's interference work (and the critic's reaction to it) does not work very well at all. First, there is basically no *Nachleben* either in the painting or in the event. Second, the technique of the squeegee was by that point in time one of Richter's well-known trademarks and in and of itself did not disrupt the spectator's expectations but rather reminded seasoned viewers of how many ways Richter had deployed the technique elsewhere to richer ends. Thus, the interference technique in this instance did not succeed in disrupting either the representational or the affective reality. Richter's 9/11 paintings, we observe sarcastically but not ironically, would work rather well on a T-shirt.

Technology and Technē (2): Chance or Indetermination?

A hallmark of a prominent strand of modern painting is its spontaneity. Whether as in the action painting of the New York abstractionists, where various modes of letting the unconscious be expressed as a means to avoid what were held to be ego structures disposed to block these deeper and freer processes, or whether in more spiritual attempts to let things happen in a Zen fashion, most closely associated with the thought and performance of John Cage, were lauded as liberating the artist from the hegemony of the ego and superego or the imagined oppressive figure of Western bourgeois consciousness.

Of these two poles, Richter, as one might expect, had familiarized himself with (and was fascinated by) Cage and his modes of deploying techniques to achieve various desubjectivizing ends. Equally, as one might expect, Richter experimented with ways to both incorporate and reject—or interfere with and redirect—both the techniques themselves and their goals. Richter takes the techniques initially developed to free the painter's primary processes and reworks those techniques so as to turn them into second-order techniques—ones that interfere with not only primary processes but with much of modernist painting. Said another way, Richter takes up several of the techniques that arose during several key turning points in modern art—various *kairos*—and deheroizes them just as he is famous for having done with photography. He is then freer to both retain and transform their effects and their capacities.

Indetermination

Aline Guillermet, in her talk at the Tate for the *Panorama* exhibit, focuses on the theme of chance, uncertainty, and mimesis. She seeks to capture what she sees as the core of Richter's experiments with chance effects in the aphorism "chance representing itself is always representation."[8]

As is well known, throughout his life Richter has kept a vast collection of photos both his own and those chosen from the mass press. These photos, arranged, and rearranged in series, are collected and displayed, presented and redisplayed in the series of publications he has called his *Atlas*. Critics have repeatedly referred to the photos as banal (often in contrast to noble or glamorous in the style of Andy Warhol). Perhaps a better term might be *ordinary*; they form a kind of archive, in part intimate in the domestic sense and in part personal in the choices the artist made of which images to preserve among the many available to him.

A selection of these photos has been used in one of Richter's distinctive subgenres: the overpainted photo. It is a subgenre because Richter also has produced overpainted prints and the like. Perhaps the best label overall is overpainted images (*Bilden*). One of the earlier techniques for combining overpainting and chance consisted in Richter selecting a photograph which he then reproduces as a print. He then takes the large blades to scrape excess paint from the squeegees he used on his canvases. The paint remaining on these scraping blades remained malleable for as long as three days. Richter began experimenting with dripping or smearing the paints remaining on the scrapers onto photoprints.

Critics have characterized this procedure as one of *chance*. The use of the term *chance* by Richter's art critics turns out to be misleading, however, as its use establishes a series of false dichotomies. For example, Guillermet's talk at the Tate stated as its problem two paradoxes in Richter's overpainted photos. The first was that there was a consistent mimetic effect between the chance overpainting and the photoprints. How, she wondered, does this harmonization take place if the application of the paint is by chance? The second paradox is how to account for Richter's use of color coordination if they are merely the effect of chance. Both paradoxes, not surprisingly, turn out to not really be paradoxes as Guillermet proceeds to demonstrate in the remainder of her talk.

For us, the term *indetermination* is a better one than *chance*. We have been testing whether the domain of indetermination is an appropriate one to identify and explore cases in the postinquiry, postactual, and contemporary. A basic advantage of the term is that it retains a thoughtful confrontation to an uncertain situation; the goal of the confrontation is to achieve a determination. In Richter's case at hand, such a determination is an overpainted photo.

Technē and Testing

Guillermet draws a distinction between a mechanical approach and one of technical manipulation. The former would be presumably a kind of method which would encompass, in one fashion or another, a wide range of examples and instances. The latter would include a technical mediation of tools and materials that would distance it from craft or the standard of consistent, machinelike regularity. Technical manipulation (or mediation) would neither eliminate the maker's choices, honed by long practice, nor would it determine the final form or allure of the made.

For Richter, the analog of the chance effects (or indetermination) that he is seeking to take account of in his own artistic practice is nature. Richter sees in nature the kind of spontaneous, arbitrary, meaningless selection processes that result nonetheless, and to a degree quite unexpectedly, in living forms and beings. Thus, Richter approaches nature in this instance not for its metaphoric value but for its techno-analogic value. What is taking place and how does it work?

Drawing on the French Nobel Prize biologist, Jacques Monod's book *Chance and Necessity*, Guillermet takes Monod's distinction between "essential chance" and "operational chance" and applies it to Richter's procedures and thinking. Essential chance in nature for Monod is the vast recombinatory processes which are not preprogrammed but which nevertheless function surprisingly effectively. Monod's example is that of the immune system where unanticipated pairings of antibodies and antigens generally protect the organism despite the fact that these encounters were not programmed prior to their activation. The comparison Guillermet draws with Richter's approach is that he is content to acknowledge that his selection process occurs only at a second-order stage; things happen (paints mix arbitrarily for the given purpose to which they are eventually put, drips drop where they may) but there is directionality to what seems to be essential chance, or primary indetermination.

The second kind of chance for Monod is "operational chance." The example is the roll of the dice or the roulette table. If, however, one manipulated the dice before rolling them, then the process would be to a degree under the control of the gamer. Not surprisingly, Guillermet observes that of course Richter knows what colors remain on the blades and therefore chooses the photos accordingly. Consequently, there is no paradox. There is a technical intervention that both establishes and resolves an indeterminate situation without that resolution being mechanically planned beforehand.

In fact, there is no paradox either in the manner in which Richter achieves mimetic effects in his overpainted photo prints; the artist notes the mottled color range left on the blades, chooses a photo that would probably have some assonance with them, and then lets the delimited technical intervention take the shape it does. If he likes the result, he keeps it; if he doesn't he reworks or discards it. In fact, it is precisely because Richter is dealing with indetermination and not chance that his choices, decisions, and artistic *phronesis* come into play.

There is, however, a further level at which a mimetic effect can work. Guillermet shows that when the overpainted photos concern nature (frequently mountainous landscapes) that there is a second affect introduced. To illustrate her point, she highlights a series of overpainted photos of the high Alps at Sils-Maria (where Nietzsche's house now has been turned into a museum). Richter was drawn to the site. The photos of snow-covered, mountain scenes in the numerous photos he took there seen by themselves could be read as almost a Romantic sense of the majesty and peace of nature, especially as the Germans appreciate and appreciated it. Once Richter overpaints them, however, a sense of motion, of disturbance, of an uncovering of another dimension to the mountain is rendered visible precisely through the absolutely nonmimetic, technological intervention of the dripped or smeared paint. This intervention not only disrupts whatever Romantic effect there might have been while marking its presence, its *Nachleben*, but produces an affect of danger, or nature's inhumanity, its uncontrollability, its foreignness.

Here we must qualify Guillermet's rather comforting claim that "chance representing itself is always representation," with a different and less comforting claim that assembling the *Nachleben* affect with a radical presence of technical painterly interference produces a second-order sense, of indetermination.

II. *Bild: Betrachtung*

Richter has created a distance between painter and viewer. In so doing, the depicted event becomes a subject of reflection.

I think he has succeeded in creating a memorial against terrorism, against ideological fanaticism.

—Hubertus Butin[9]

In the ever-expanding, almost uniquely art historical secondary literature on Gerhard Richter, critics have focused the core of their analytic and critical attention on Richter's technique of blurring worked-over photographic images, his family paintings taken up as nostalgic domestic throwbacks or troubling portrayals of his family's Nazi past, the complicated status of his vast production of his so-called abstract images, the meaning of his frequent change of medium, and, perhaps above all, the significance of his October 18, 1977, group with its series of painted images of the deaths of members of the Red Army Faction. In sum, on the one hand, the critical literature has mainly concentrated on Richter's diverse techniques and, on the other hand, a smaller body of commentary takes up the artist's work and life in representational terms addressing what they interpret as content and significance of Richter's images work and the reasons for the inclusion of that content and its underlying and unifying significance.

As to the ratio of praise to blame, whether tacit or explicit, art critics and cultural commentators have sustained almost without exception a questioning attitude rather than a judgmental one: what exactly is Richter doing in this or that canvas, this or that series? It is only occasionally, and often not without a certain caution whose tone expresses a sense that one might be missing the point, that critics offer explicit judgments as to either the quality or the meaning of an instance of Richter's work. In our vocabulary, we claim that Richter's critics and commentators have operated mainly in the domain of the *indeterminate* rather than the *discordant*.

Thus, sustainable judgments as to whether Richter and/or his work are good or bad, successful or unsuccessful, meaningful or not, politically right wing or left wing are sparse. There are occasional explicit bits of praise (like the one in the epigram above) but these are more throwaway lines than supportable evaluations. Whether for strategic reasons or not, throughout his career Gerhard Richter has made himself widely available to critics and commentators; this affable availability and the quality and range of Richter's work seems to have kept many critics off guard and seemingly simply reticent to make nuanced evaluations of his work. Given how uninhibited in its judgments the art critical world is habitually, and given its attachments to current theory in the academy with its strong historical and political perspectives, as well as the value-laden global art market, whatever Richter's techniques are for escaping more skeptical scrutiny should be marked by cultural observers as worthy of more attention.

Granted Richter has neither endorsed nor elaborated specific criteria to identify success or failure in his work. For example, in the film *Gerhard Richter Painting*, we see several scenes of Richter pondering his freshly painted canvases acknowledging to the offscreen questioner that he is not yet sure whether they are done or not, successful or not, whether they please him or not. In the film, Richter's assistants attest to the fact that he not infrequently changes his mind about the status and quality of a painting over the course of short periods of time (days, weeks)—at times leaving it untouched after initially expressing uncertainty or hesitation or even approval about its status; at other times entirely painting over a canvas; or at yet other times making either minor alterations or else major squeegee and/or color alterations to either parts or to the canvas as a whole. Only the master knows for sure and he is not always so sure.

The exception that proves the rule are the interpretations of Richter developed by Kaja Silverman whose psychoanalytic and feminist readings, although provocative and contestable, seem to have elicited little published response from other critics. For example, the claims and interpretive criteria put forth at her keynote presentation at the Tate symposium at the opening of the *Panorama* exhibit stood in stark opposition to a number of other presentations (including one of the exhibit's organizers, Mark Godfrey). Silverman's central interpretive strategy has been to analyze Richter as working through unresolved psychological relationships with his own past, present, and future. The nature of the evidence presented to support her interpretations differed in kind from the other presentations. Specifically, Silverman assigned semantic meaning to technique (for example, downward brushstrokes) thereby making it available for a hermeneutics of suspicion when convenient, while similar instances of techniques such as downward brush strokes in other paintings have been left unmentioned. In sum, Silverman's attempt to provide a totalizing framework for Richter's life and work by combining the political and the therapeutic in a manner that is totalizing and reveals the deep meaning available only to the interpretive gaze is modernist to the hilt. Not coincidentally, her interpretations are cast in an ironic mood; naturally this claim does not mean they are wrong (although we think they are) but that they are not contemporary ones.

During the question period that followed Silverman's presentation (and that is included on the video on the Richter website), one could sense that not everyone was convinced but basically no direct engagement with her views took place, at least in public. The event was taking place in Britain after all, and everyone was on good behavior.

A Memorial, Not a Contemporary Image

As should be clear by now, we are not attempting here to develop an aesthetic that would provide a comprehensive framework within which to understand and to evaluate Richter's paintings or for that matter his writings or his life. Rather, we have taken up parts of Richter's work and the critical apparatus that has developed around it as an instance which provides us the opportunity to test the parameters we have developed so as to explore and check the terms of a contemporary mood and mode.

One way to understand Butin's quote, "Richter has created a distance between painter and viewer. In so doing, the depicted event becomes a subject
of reflection," is that it is a renewed assertion for the relevance of the traditional function of art: moral uplift or civic lessons, exemplary figuration
of persons or scenes, or most broadly the function of art as a pedagogical
Bildung.

As we have seen (and can agree with), Butin himself makes a compelling
case earlier in the same lecture in which the above claim appears that Richter's "candle" paintings cannot and must not be taken as direct imitations or
repetitions of the *vanitas* genre. Rather, Richter's overpainting of such figural
images is designed to produce an interference with attempts to understand
the paintings as merely continuous with this older iconographic lineage.
Nonetheless, Richter can be seen to be deploying one variant of the function
of *Nachleben* that not only puts into question the traditional understandings
of these images but modernist ones as well that would negate the former
affect and significance entirely. It follows that to the degree this work of
interference and reassemblage "works" (for the artist and/or for a projected
viewer), then the affect produced would be one of pathos. The form would
both affirm and deny the tradition and its negation, leaving open the question of what remains to be worked with and over today.

Such *Pathosaffekt* functions on a number of levels. First, for the artist it
provides a test of how to facilitate the ratio of technique and *technē*. The
range of possible topics or themes susceptible to be treated as such in a
crucible of testing would be vast. Consequently the artist is obliged to make
choices as to which theme he is drawn to explore and test himself with, and
how to decide on a specific topic in the large thematic field. In the genre of
moral lessons in art, Richter has chosen the topic of *vanitas*. As with the Romantics' connection to nature, which Richter felt free to take up once again
because there was no danger, if the proper *technē* was deployed, of simply
returning to that earlier position of viewing or understanding. So, too, it
seems, taking up the theme of the futility and effervescence of worldly pursuits can be explored by Richter. Butin's earlier analysis showed how Richter
achieves the work of the image; the explicit stylistic inclusion of *Nachleben*,
and the forging of a form that fits and renders visible the pathos of such an
image, we claim, makes the image a contemporary one.

As concerns Butin's other claim that Richter has succeeded in the 9/11
painting in creating "a memorial against terrorism and against ideological
fanaticism," one would be likely to agree. As we will see, however, Mark
Godfrey makes a compelling case that the very power, richness, and original-
ity of Richter's images when they "work" consisted in his vigilant negative

anticipation of images that might be taken as memorials. Consequently, to the extent that Richter's 9/11 painting (and the preparatory sketches) functions as an explicit memorial, it is a failure.

Finally, we must examine Butin's claim that "Richter has created a distance between painter and viewer. In so doing, the depicted event becomes a subject of reflection." Each aspect of the claim may well be valid for the 9/11 painting. To the degree that it does apply, however, it is precisely that validity that exempts the painting from being considered as either successful or contemporary. One must be grateful however, to this serious critic for opening a question that has received scant attention: What is the place of the observer (if it is not one of a fixed distance that provides for reflection on an event)?

In sum, we think that the fixed relation that Butin claims Richter is providing between the observer and the image in his 9/11 painting may well be there. To the degree they are achieved, however, is the degree, we argue that the painting is not successful. To the degree that Richter's image (*Bild*) activates or motivates or induces a *Bildung* of reflection on terrorism and ideological fanaticism is the degree to which the painting becomes an illustration.

War Cut

> I absolutely avoided expressing an opinion, which is completely useless here and obstructs the attempt to come somewhat closer to the truth. In addition, my opinion is almost certainly just as wrong as that of my friends who almost all greatly simplify matters, condemning the war and grumbling about Bush in a way that is closer to Kitsch. That is not my way.
>
> —Gerhard Richter [10]

Critics, most prominently Robert Storr who had been one of Richter's main interlocutors during the 1990s and who brought the *October 17, 1977* paintings to the Museum of Modern Art which eventually acquired them, produced an entire monograph situating the 9/11 paintings within Richter's oeuvre.[11] Storr included a chapter that framed the monograph in light of his own reactions to the attack on the twin towers as he was in Brooklyn at the time. He assigns significance to the fact that Richter and his wife were flying to New York for an opening on 9/11 when their plane was forced to land in Canada and ultimately to return to Germany. Although it took Richter until 2005 to begin to work on a painting about 9/11 and although the artist suffered only a minor inconvenience during the event, Storr ascribes the painting expressive and existential content of a direct referential sort. Kaja Silverman also interprets the painting as personally significant, providing a complex psychoanalytic reading that includes a reference to a remark Richter made on a trip to New York decades earlier about wanting to blow up the city.

Richter's book-length assemblage, *War Cut*, catalyzed by the American invasion of Iraq in 2003, provides an informative contrast with the 9/11 painting and the interpretations given to it. The *War Cut* book consists of a large abstract painting Richter had done a long time previously which he subsequently photographed and reproduced in multiple small images. For *War Cut* he collated these smaller images with sections of articles from the German press that appeared during the initial days of the American invasion.

In an interview in 2004, Richter framed the work as follows:

JAN THORN-PRIKKER: Can you say something about the abstract painting that served as a starting point for *War Cut*?

GERHARD RICHTER: That picture was done years ago in the 1980s, so the Iraq war wasn't involved. I was slightly surprised when the Musée d'Art Moderne de la Ville de Paris bought the picture; there are more attractive works, not so rough and harsh. But about two years ago I took close-ups of the work in the museum without knowing what I might use them for. When the war started, I heard all these conflicting opinions. I thought newspaper reports were salutary—ineffectual and impotent as everything else, in the face of tragedy—but their plain presentation of the facts consoled me.

Richter is clear that the images have no representational relation to events in the Middle East, whether in Iraq or elsewhere. Richter is also clear that the original image had no affective relation to war.

The direct referential dimension of *War Cut* to war and to the events surrounding the American invasion is present in the interspaced clippings from the German press. Here, too, however, Richter is not deploying them as commentary:

JT-P: Do you include all the articles published about the Iraq war in the paper on the first two days, or did you leave some out?

GR: I left some out. My layout determined what I included or did not include. It was not something I had specifically in mind before I started. . . . But the specific arrangement evolved as I worked on it, until at some stage there were 324 pages. I read most of the texts only after I placed them with the pictures. I read them as literature which was very pleasing. I was not looking for straight-forward narrative, which is also maybe why I chose that particular abstract painting. . . . The picture was close to being non-communicative, which I don't mean negatively.

Although the invasion and the reactions in the press and among his circle of acquaintances triggered an emotional reaction in Richter, he is clear that what is present in *War Cut* was neither the emotion he experienced in its raw and personal state, nor an opinion on the events. Richter expressed contempt for those who might claim that being a celebrated artist would somehow have given his personal views special political weight or import.

Rather, Richter set to work to meet the demands of the day in his own manner:

JT-P: Would you say something about the unusual form of *War Cut*?
GR: My approach to form is very simple. Whatever is real is so unlimited and unshaped that we have to summarize it. The more dramatic the events are, the more important the form.
Form is all we have to cope with fundamentally chaotic facts and assaults.
Formulating something is a great start.

In our vocabulary we can hear Richter saying that the challenge for the artist was to move from the present to the contemporary, avoiding the lure of the actual with its warranted propositions or its vindicatory subject position. Artwork requires its own specific form of testing and checking.

We find evidence for our interpretation of this motion from the present to the contemporary as a hard-won practice in working in a crucible under controlled conditions in Richter's arch reply to his interviewer's question as to whether his form building was a chance development:

As for chance consider John Cage. His musical compositions were never a to-tal appropriation of a chance acoustic event. He devised an ingenious system to build structures from dumb abundance. And he devoted even more skill to giving form to this succession of sounds. That is the absolute opposite of chance, nature and rubbish.

Having to dot the proverbial "i's" and cross the proverbial "t's," it should be clear by now that Richter is neither providing any identifiable space for the viewer to comfortably occupy nor opening a stable and recognizable space for reflection.

Undaunted, the interviewer, no doubt sensing correctly that his reader-
ship would not be satisfied with the range of Richter's answers, pushed him
once again to provide a political or personal account of the work's genesis
or meaning.

JT-P: Your book is contradictory. As an artist's work it says, "That's how things
are. That's how the world looks." However the same book simultaneously
says, "That's unacceptable. Things can't continue like this." The book both
raises a protest against the world as it is and confirms that state of affairs.
GR: Yes, that is also why I wanted to try and see this war from a completely different angle. Admonitions, protests and such are not my thing.[12]

Dissatisfied with this answer, he pressed on.

JT-P: Does the fact that you belong to the generation that experienced World War
II influence your feelings about war?
GR: Yes, these experiences are present like an underlying theme.[13]

At last, partially satisfied that there was an identifiable personal and historical connection of the artist that other Germans could relate to—and
which the interviewer pursued at length with Richter in a subsequent interview—he pressed on.

JT-P: Was this a way of expressing sympathy?
GR: Yes, it is. But the greatest pleasure was to complete this book. Then it was fun
to have produced something beautiful. I found my way back to painting. That
was a new beginning after a long intermission. After all, I hadn't painted for
two years. It was good to produce something like this. Something story-like,
something fantastic. The absolute opposite of war.[14]

Consequently, Richter was neither producing a memorial nor depicting an
event so as to make it a subject of reflection for viewers. Rather, he was
creating a form in which temporality would neither be frozen nor historicity denied without resorting to referentiality. Richter included referential
elements (the press clippings) and then interfered with their original form
while extracting as it were and transfiguring dimensions of their affective
import.

    In sum, we argue that if there were a subject of reflection present in *War
Cut*, it was the results of a process of testing whether or not a second-order
form-giving could be rendered contemporary. Did it succeed? Only if one

accepts a *Pathosformel*, saturated with *Nachleben*, derived from a long distant *kairos* and the affect and consternation they produced.

III. Contemporary Parameters

The contemporary is a moving ratio of modernity, moving through the recent past and near future in a (nonlinear) space that gauges modernity as an ethos already becoming historical.

—Paul Rabinow[15]

Mark Godfrey, one of the Tate Modern curators of the 2011–2012 exhibition *Gerhard Richter, Panorama, a Retrospective,* in his fine presentation, *A Curtain of Trees,* provides compelling insights into the background and meaning to a series of Richter's experiments. As we find Godfrey's insights convincing (albeit too extended if they were to be taken to apply to all of Richter's paintings of nature), we take his topics up as vital parameters of Richter's art of the contemporary.[16]

The first such topic is that for Richter "affect is more important than imagery."[17] Richter should not be approached, Godfrey argues, at a literal level of iconography. He is not a painter whose work contains a hidden significance carried directly in the images themselves. As is well known, Richter very frequently paints in series and his final images are always altered from their original state: be it directly representational, once removed as in photography, or multiply removed and transformed via his imagination, technique, and *technē.*

The second topic that Godfrey introduces and addresses is formulated as a problem: "Could one make a radical painting from a traditional image?" We modify this formulation by asking the following: Given the presence of a long history of images, some of which now qualify within the art historical discipline as traditional, how can they be taken up in a contemporary manner? Phrased in our technical language, given the inescapability of *Nachleben* for those aware of them, and not methodically refusing their presence or actuality, what are the techniques and *technē* available to give them a contemporary form?

The third of Godfrey's topics is a claim: "No matter what the desire for continuity with the past, one is left with a consciousness of a break that makes cohesion impossible."[18] The citation he provides is to an essay by Theodor Adorno. This claim might well be pursued in a narratively tragic mood that constantly admonished both the maker and the observer to never forget the fundamental and irrevocable discontinuity between past and present. Equally, however, Godfrey's claim could be taken up in a mood of pathos in which the partial success in achieving relations between past and present motivates one to test whether such relations have been achieved, how they endure and how and when they break down, and what are the available technologies of repair for the artist.

The fourth topic in Godfrey's presentation is that the point of painting is to seek to render visible things that are "unknowable and unrepresentable."[19] This argument does not mean that painting is impossible or thoroughly imaginary. Rather it means that there are domains that are not available to discourse (énoncés). Such domains, furthermore, are not things or images or forms that can be captured through representations. The challenge of art is to render visible aspects of such a domain.

One consistent technique that Richter employs to ward off direct representation is to confront it head-on and to interfere with it. Thus, his numerous paintings of clouds, or seas or, for that matter, cities incite an initial representational response which is then undercut, disaggregated, reduced, or disrupted so as to make visible among other things the materiality of the paint, the collage effects underlying what had seemed initially to be realistic, the diverse visibilities available depending on how close or how far one stands in viewing. Such techniques contribute to a techne for all concerned which obliges an acknowledgment of how things are known and seen and how knowing and seeing renders images shapely.

One of the problems of an array of techniques that Richter has experimented with over the years is the following: "How to treat color in a painting not as a compositional element?"[20] Such a technical problem is also a problem of techne. It should be a problem for critics as well although it frequently is not. Not only do some critics have a recourse to a hermeneutics of color, others, proceeding more cautiously and professionally in a disciplinary sense, present detailed discourses on how color, or brush strokes, or other such practical aspects of a painting are to be read as the keys or at least central elements to the form.

Finally, Godfrey presents the topic: "How could the practice of painting continue without subjective content?"[21] To the degree that Godfrey is correct in assessing Richter as accepting and experimenting with solutions to this problem, then, once again, those critics who "read" Richter's painting almost exclusively in terms of their intentionality, their subjective content, for either or both painter and viewer, are themselves falling into the fallacy of taking up painting as the object of an inquiry or a symptom of the painter or the epoch.

Kairos: *A Curtain of Trees*

Although Richter has been labeled by Buchloh and others as a Romantic, a label Richter always refuses, it might actually seem more appropriate to label him an anti-Romantic in the French line of Baudelaire or Huysmans, best known for his book *A Rebours, Against the Grain*. Both are in the dandy tradition of ironic modernism in which the social and the natural are reworked, after close observation, against the grain. Nature for Huysman is raw material to be reutilized and given style. Huysman's novel recounts the production of strange plants with unexpected colors, tortoises as household robots, and the like. In any case, these nineteenth-century moderns sought to heighten the present to a point of such acuity that its absurdity and arbitrariness are rendered visible. Their maxim might well have been, "You have no right to despise the present, even if all these bourgeois are dressed to attend a funeral." It is the present that is brought to a breaking point; there is no history in a genealogical or scholarly sense to be dealt with even if for Baudelaire that which he sees comes from a long line of degradation and the occasional flash of beauty from the depraved animal.[22]

One of those critical of how Richter takes up nature is Benjamin Buchloh, the art historian and longtime friend of Richter, who Richter refers to in the film as "my teacher," accuses Richter, in an agonistic manner (buffered by their friendship), of being a Romantic. In a famous 1986 interview, Buchloh confronts Richter with what he takes to be a mirror in which Richter has no utopian vision of society to balance and counteract Richter's Romantic vision of nature.[23] To the extent this charge carries weight it would mean that Richter was a conservative in the artistic and presumably political sense.

As Mark Godfrey points out in his Tate lecture, "A Curtain of Trees," Buchloh's portrayal has carried much weight among the practitioners of art criticism. Godfrey argues that there is a lineage of modernist criticism of abstract art that is vigilant about refusing the introduction, discursive or otherwise, of external referentiality per se and especially reference, analogy, or metaphor bridges to nature. He quotes Rosalind Krauss's essay attacking those who saw a Jackson Pollack painting entitled *Lavender Mist* as being "about" rain; the title (perhaps given by a gallery owner) is an unfortunate bit of irony that could only mislead those in search of figuration, as well as those operating in anything but an ironic mood.[24] The dogma of high modernism was that painting was about painting: the practice, the material, at best the oblique references to an internal tradition of those who came before in the recent past. Godfrey closes the first part of his lecture by wondering (and obviously the rest of the lecture will provide a nuanced answer): "What if Richter's approach to the natural is inseparable from his approach to history?"

Godfrey, like his superior at the Tate Nicolas Serota, produces an excursus on technique in Richter, specifically his use of downward strokes on the canvas, only to leave it behind (having demonstrated his authority as an art historian and curator). He then returns to the Richter-Buchloh interview of 1986 in which Richter responds to Buchloh's agonistic labeling with a ferocious return thrust, "Nature is brutal, meaningless, inhumane, mindless, etc." At least of the level of his intentions, Gerhard Richter did not see himself as either a reactionary or a Romantic.

Godfrey begins to answer his rhetorical question in what follows. He asks: "Where did this brutal image of nature come from?" His answer: the Nazi extermination camps. The camps were set in the German and Polish countryside. Godfrey shows opening clips from Alain Resnais' *Night and Fog* and Claude Lansmann's *Shoah*, the two greatest cinematic attempts to confront the Holocaust. In both there is an idyllic image of the countryside, befitting the modernist contempt for the evocation of the "merely landscape." Thereafter, remaining remnants of the pastoral are shattered.

Of the remarkably rare photographic images of the extermination camps during their time of gruesome workings, a blank hole in the twentieth century's ever-expanding avalanche of images, there is one of a copse of birch trees outside of the eponymously named Birkenau camp. The art historian, Georges Didi-Huberman, in the article Godfrey is drawing from, "Images Despite It All," refers to "a curtain of trees around the camp."[25]

These rare photographs were taken surreptitiously by a member of the *Sondercommanden*, the Jewish guards who survived by working in the camps for the Nazis, keeping order, and performing tasks such as burying the remains of the cremated. One existing photo of special significance is blurred (presumably hurriedly taken from the hip) and is grayish in tone. Didi-Huberman draws an analogy between the gray of the photograph and the gray of the cinders, remains of those cremated, in the furnaces. Richter himself, and the critical literature following his lead, have given much attention to Richter's use of gray. Among other qualities, Richter has periodically in his career (and life) praised gray for its meaninglessness and its neutrality.

Godfrey then turns in his lecture to Richter's *Atlas* in which concentration camp photos were first collected by the artist. They were placed adjacent to ordinary pornographic images from German magazines of the time (1950s). Richter was contemplating exhibiting both types of images together but decided against it at the last minute. Again, much critical commentary takes up these images in the *Atlas*.

Although he backed away from a public exhibition, Richter did return to the photos of the camps. He decided to color parts of the black-and-white photos by tinting a few areas, a gesture that he has not explained. Godfrey offers a compelling interpretation: following an insight from Jean-Francois Lyotard that "once fixed, memories can be forgotten." Hence the tinting can be seen plausibly as an immediate gesture of defamiliarization, blocking, or interfering with the affective mood of viewing these by now familiar if still terrible photos. Furthermore, the tinting can be seen plausibly as a marking that blocks or defers the images from becoming a memorial.

Godfrey concludes that for Richter, nature is bound up with these images of the curtain of trees, the forest, the landscape, and cultivated fields that form the frame for the camps. This unsettling connection is especially true for Birkenwald. There is a photo of this "forest of birches" on the wall in Richter's studio (it also appears in the film). The photo is taken from some distance away. In it one can see several figures who appear to be tending to nature, perhaps cleaning up leaves; they appear at first glance, Richter observes to Serota in another interview, as if they were "nice gardeners." That first impression turns out to be an appalling mistake, perhaps a residue of our habituation to impressionist and postimpressionist views of landscapes or the ever-present snapshots of the countryside. In fact, the photo is an image of *Sonderkommanden* burying corpses. For Richter, the forests, rivers, and fields are haunted by what must be oxymoronically named *Nachleben*, survivals of death in all their brutality, and inhumanity.

Finally, Godfrey turns to a series of twelve paintings Richter undertook in 1990 with the series title of *Wald*, woods. These are paintings of darkness and concealment. He concludes that the forest or woods which once stood for a protected space, a sanctuary, and a home can no longer retain such a univocal meaning any more than those meanings left over from the Romantics. "The woods are a very different place now."

Reproach, Response: Philia + Agōn

Reproach: That type of objection which if one accepts to defend oneself against it traps one into fatally subscribing to the terms that the reproaches uphold.

Reproches, c'est-à-dire les objections qui sont telles qu'à s'en défendre, on souscrit fatalement à ce qu'elles soutiennent.

—Michel Foucault[26]

One of the distinctive and striking aspects of Gerhard Richter's production is the amount of prose that he has produced, singularly or in multiple interviews, and publications. This production is striking, because Richter himself seems somewhat shy and not especially articulate. Furthermore, he often disagrees with the interviewer's interpretations of his work. One might suppose that these interviews and exchanges of letters and the like are simply a means for Richter to be social, to clarify his thoughts, to respond to critics and the like. It is probably the case that all of the above apply. The question remains: Why publish all of this material?

One simple reason is that Richter is a man of order; just like his cataloguing of his prodigious production, the periodic updating of his *catalogue raisonnée* with inclusions and exclusions, Richter keeps track of things. But why make this public? One reason is that it facilitates the sale of his work; by this point in his life Gerhard Richter must be an extremely rich man. A recent auction sold one of his abstract paintings for the highest price ever received by a living artist.[27] Richter is a bourgeois, living in a spacious compound of house and studio, presumably supporting his current and past wives and his children. For a long time now he has employed assistants in the studio as well as a business staff, glimpses of whom can be seen in the film *Gerhard Richter Painting*. He has an archivist.

Perhaps most striking of all, he is quite open about this, and although he appears (or presents himself) as modest and unpretentious, open to encounters and public appearances not to mention a continuous flow of exhibitions which he supervises and attends, he has not objected to being called with some regularity "the most important living artist."[28]

Paradoxically enough, perhaps this unabashed embodiment of high bourgeois lifestyle with its celebration of domesticity and the like is one of his most iconoclastic features. Just as Richter asserts that there is no reason why he cannot return to and learn from German Romantic painting without being a German Romantic painter, so too, he is breaking the mold of the modern painter, the antibourgeois, bohemian, often mysterious and/or self-destructive artist. There is not a hint of Faust, or Dr. Faustus, in the narratives concerning Gerhard Richter.

In a publication entitled "Notes 1989" (March 14th) Richter writes:

> The word "bourgeois," formerly a compliment, now negative in its connotations, much used, always vaguely polemical, jejune and irrelevant. "Bourgeois" equals tidy, educated, law-abiding, in contrast to flipped-out, cheerfully dressed, ostentatiously nonconformist (e.g. Thomas Mann as against Bertolt Brecht, President Weizsacker as against Joschka Fisher).

Just as conformism is not all the same thing as security—the word denotes a deference to prevailing fashions, and to the prevailing climate or system, which springs from stupidity, cowardice, indolence and baseness—nonconformism is not necessarily its diametrical opposite, but often springs from a courage born of stupidity and blindness. Nonconformist laxity often originates in the confined, retarded structure of mindless insolence.[29]

There is, however, a pronounced restiveness. Richter is self-critical and self-aware. He has developed an insistent *technē* of working, reworking, observing, revisiting, and at times destroying his paintings. Although there is nothing unusual about that per se, Richter, while encouraging response and informed criticism, rarely seems to overtly agree with it. He rather frequently ironizes. His self-characterization of how he knows whether a painting is finished or good is cryptic. His assistants who appear in the film make equally hesitant evaluations of how Richter decides something is done. They remark that he returns to paintings he had expressed admiration for and at times redoes them; or the opposite.

Therefore, when Richter does respond to criticism it is worth paying attention to what irked him. In a letter entitled "Letter to Walter Grasskamp on the Subject of *18 October 1977*," dated October 17, 1989, Richter responds in part:

> I could just dismiss all of this as helpless rubbish, but the painful thing about it is that you entangle your thinking in strategic categories, that you accuse me of your own purely tactical political sense, and in doing so you undermine any attempt I could make to clarify to you my actual motivations. Following this train of thought it's only natural that you come to the determination that the death of the RAF members I was interested in can only be seen as the "expression of a political—and therefore quite abstract—failure." It seems apparent, though, there is something "quite abstract" about you, particularly when I see now your discomfort with "covert radicalism." I must tell you that I have never strived for radicalism (something I have stated publicly on several occasions) because as a matter of fact I have other concerns. In the same way, the question of whether I am making history paintings or not could hardly be less important to me.
>
> However, I consider not quite so unimportant your false accusation that the paintings allow the viewer "to read into them anything he wants"—because even if you saw the paintings as nothing more than a catalogue of reproductions, surely you would have imagined a huge list of everything that was not visible in them.

And then at the same time you do find a way to claim something is lacking: for example, in the case of Hanns Martin Schleyer: "the photos of his disintegration as a hostage" and "the ghostly shots of the crime scene with the corpse of the driver and the bodyguards." Sure, that sounds really striking, but it is a patently malicious misrepresentation of the theme of my work, which you go on to accuse me of making it "seem as if the government had driven" the terrorists "to their death." Don't even you yourself think that's a bit mean?

And at the end of all this you are "taken aback." Suspicion arises in you because certain photos of individuals were not allowed to be reproduced (for the protection of family members) and because I did not wish to have the paintings sold on the art market.

I can only view these suspicions as abject and cynical; and, in comparison, all your other misrepresentations become irrelevant—even the hair-raising nonsense that I paint solely "pictures of pictures," and never of reality. This is nothing more than appalling high-school art theory.

Perhaps you'll notice that in taking issue here, if ever so briefly, I've actually grappled with your article; while for your part, instead of criticizing the paintings, you merely speculated about motivations and imputed strategies, thus denouncing the work.[30]

On the one hand, this exchange (or the part of it we have) can readily be seen as an example of why the bourgeois/nonconformist binary is so dated. It is deployed here against Richter as a polemic that pigeonholes everything he has done to "appalling high-school art theory." On the other hand, and of more interest, is the fact that Richter had been attacked on both the right and the left with polemic assaults marked by their utter assurance of the intent and meanings of the paintings. Ultimately Richter sold the paintings to the Museum of Modern Art in New York rather than the Frankfurt museums (where these events had taken place). This act equally aroused indignation.

The two charges that Richter angrily answers in the above letter are that anyone can read anything into his paintings; and that he does not paint reality. Richter seems aroused to self-justification, although he only offers a bare minimum (that he did not want to put other families in danger, etc.) To arrive at a full vindicatory position, one might expect, would have required a ringing and elaborate explanation of how to see the paintings. And while it is true that in other interviews Richter does provide aspects of such instructions and explanations, perhaps the basic act of *vindication* (in the double sense of the term) was his act to sell the paintings to MOMA. Let them be seen as paintings (the Americans after all were not familiar with the details of the RAF when it happened and certainly not decades later). Perhaps by so doing, Richter joins a long and distinguished list of Germans who exiled themselves, for a time, to the United States (Thomas Mann, Bertolt Brecht, Theodor Adorno, etc.).

Beyond Reproach

Richter is no hermit or artistic purist above the fray. As mentioned, his writings and practices were complexly engaged with a range of critics of multiple kinds.

BENJAMIN BUCHLOH: Why have you so firmly rejected any concrete political intention in your art?

GR: Because politics does not suit me, because art has an entirely different function, because all I can do is paint. Call it conservative.

BB: But by limiting yourself to the medium of painting, might not you be espousing not just a conservative position but maybe also a critical dimension? Are you, for instance, calling into question the immediacy claimed by work like that of Beuys?

GR: Naturally, by limiting myself to painting I imply a criticism of a lot of things that I don't like, not all of them connected with painting.

BB: So you don't deny on principle that someone might validly intend to make a critical political statement through art?

GR: I probably do deny it. But what counts is that I have to ask as my starting point, my foundation, my own possibilities, and my own premises.[31]

In another interview with Buchloh in 2004, we include the following snippets:[32]

BB: So, you are the last great painter?

GR: When you put it that way, I don't know how else to answer.

BB: Do you believe that painting is really about the preservation of masterful, individualist, artisanal production? Or don't you much rather think that it's about the conceptual, cognitive, and perceptual foundations of the work of art, which can be saved in paintings?

GR: It all fits together, though.

BB: Well, isn't it what you want to preserve there this extreme ambiguity of your work, a contradictoriness unimaginable for anyone else, which really can only be produced by painterly means?

GR: No, it could be produced by other means as well. For my *Panes of Glass*, the same criteria apply as I use in judging a painting by Chardin.

BB: What about when, in the present moment, you paint the structure of silicate?

GR: In the end it doesn't matter what I paint, it is always about the same quality.

BB: So, it's more about a specific definition of the differentiated subjectivity, not specific techniques that need to be rescued?

GR: I would never want to rescue a technique.

BB: What makes you so confident?

GR: Even the present has moments of promise.

Checking the Contemporary

I think philosophic askēsis should be understood as a certain way of constituting the subject of true knowledge as the subject of right action. And in constituting oneself as the subject of true knowledge and right action, one situates oneself within or takes as the correlate of oneself, a world that is perceived, recognized and practiced as a test.

—Michel Foucault[1]

Our problem has been to undertake the process of addressing the question of how to practice anthropology in a contemporary manner. One reason that we identify this challenge as a problem is that clearly we cannot return to the practice of Stoic philosophy from which Foucault genealogically articulated the problem of truth and conduct. Equally we cannot return to the Kantian pragmatic anthropology not only because of the complex and dependent place it held within his transcendental and critical philosophy; but even more because his framing of the pragmatic as a cosmo-political frame and task was set within a view of providence and history that however chastened Kant held it to be at the end of the Enlightenment is today but a fading memory, a topic of regret as the Stoics would have it. Finally, John Dewey's modern pragmatic philosophy has offered us many valuable concepts and terms. Dewey, however, posited a horizon of the ultimate work of philosophy as reconstruction, the forging of intellectual instrumentalities that would bring what he hoped would be a more fully human understanding and practice into being. As we have explained here and elsewhere, we find little hope or enlightenment in holding to the metric of reconstruction or its diminished derivatives. Michel Foucault gave us the contours of the general problem of truth and conduct, as well as the key indicator that the work to be done turned on the creation of forms and the practices that would bring them into being rather than simply remain as ideas or values. He died before he could extend his work beyond his brilliant genealogical forays, assuming that he would have taken that direction.

Anthropology, since its foundation as a modern scholarly discipline over a century ago, has based itself on the practice of fieldwork. That practice has been justified either in terms of an existential initiation (which, it has been held, yields credibility to the claim of ethnographic authority) or its scientific contribution to one or another subfield of the discipline (kinship, symbolic anthropology, religion, law, area studies, etc.). More recently field-work and reports from the field have been justified as political.

When anthropology is practiced philosophically, a number of different things happen. The practice remains a form of existential initiation as long as a disciplined form of self-observation is put to the test as both experience and thought. By so doing, individual subjectivity or the practice as a form of individual therapy are demoted. Second, the goal of contribution to a scientific formation is once again given prominence but not in its positiv-ist or merely empirical form. Rather, a demonstration of experimental de-sign, diagnosis, conceptual repertoire, problem specification, and resulting determinations cast as warranted assertions is set out as a pragmatic goal. The achievement of the latter only results after the existential initiation, the work and labor of the experiment, and—crucially—the labor of the concept that follows fieldwork. Such labor must itself be the subject and object of conceptual scrutiny. What are produced are a certain distance and a certain disinterestedness from the experiences of the field.

There are probing resonances with a series of aphorisms in Theodor Adorno's *Minima Moralia*. We find an arresting assonance with our own thought in aphorism number 82, "Keeping one's distance." Adorno writes:

> Only at a remove from life can the mental life exist, and truly engage the empirical.[2]

Although this claim could be taken as a call for contemplation, obviously the Frankfurt thinker was not advocating that kind of remove from what is being observed and is challenging one's thought. He adds:

> Distance is not a safety-zone but a field of tension. It is manifested not in relaxing the claim of ideas to truth, but in delicacy and fragility of thinking.[3]

We have previously identified the position an anthropological observer should occupy as one of *adjacency*.

Whatever exactly Adorno is affirming for his own thought, we can concur that not relaxing conceptual rigor and its warrant through inquiry is mandatory. Although it is hard to decide precisely what Adorno meant by the "delicacy and fragility of thinking," we can take up this trope up and translate it as a diacritic quality of the contemporary mode and mood. The term *delicacy* turns on a quality of thought and the weight one gives to it as one's practicing interpretive analytics is hard to pin down but certainly must be related to a form of *phronesis* that is an earned sensibility of those who have long practiced inquiry and the arts of vindicatory thought.

We can give the term *fragility* a more specific translation. For us, the fragility or, better, *brittleness* of one's interpretations of the contemporary turns on the practice of testing (to use the English translator's equivalent of Foucault's semantically richer *épreuve*) or, at least in some situations it is better to call it *checking*. The term *brittle* combines a quality of stress and one of relative capacity to respond to or stand up against what one might best call 'checking,' when one is referring to interpretations of a contemporary case taken up in a contemporary mode. The sense we are trying to capture here is sharpened by thinking of the propositions that are produced and warranted in the process of inquiry. Such determinations are obviously not meant to be infallible, but as they have already been put to a number of stress tests during the experimental stage of inquiry they may well be (and should be) contestable but they should not be brittle as they have already been hardened, as it were, in the crucible of the actual.

In the same aphorism Adorno continues,

> If instead of interpretation it seeks to become mere statement, everything it states becomes, in fact, untrue.[4]

In the practice of the contemporary reverting to ideas or values as self-evident or declarations of what is, renders them into claims about the *actual* for us and by so doing changes the register and domain of how to evaluate them.

Aphorism number 83 is cryptically entitled "Vice-President."[5] It begins with a *paraskeuē*-like admonition, "Advice to intellectuals, let no-one represent you."[6] Our cases have provided ample material to check this advice; Richter seems to have internalized it from the outset of his career and Rushdie learned the weight of its wisdom during the long course of his trials and tribulations as he endured a series of those seeking to represent him, not coincidentally including various self-justificatory avatars he performed himself.

Whatever political effect such scientific or artistic work may have is indirect. The anthropologist may decide to become an activist or continue her activism in light of what has been learned anthropologically. The anthropologist may decide to work as an expert for other organizations whose aims she shares. Or, finally, the anthropologist may choose to restylize herself as an intellectual, general in the manner of one who speaks truth to power.

We have pursued another path which is neither therapeutic nor political in a direct manner. Rather, it is a kind of philosophy understood as a persistent practice of anthropology and anthropology understood as a persistent practice of philosophy. The practice is philosophical insofar as it foregrounds various forms of truth and conduct as a problem and a check on what one is doing. The practice is anthropological insofar as it insists on disciplined and engaged inquiry as a prerequisite. The practice prepares one to engage the topology of the contemporary when the philosophic checks have been tested in a sustained manner and when the anthropological inquiry has been warranted and vindicated.

Contemporary Soundings

There is a final unexpected assonance between Adorno's compact phrasing and our own thought. At the end of "Keeping one's distance," aphorism number 82, Adorno writes, "The distance of thought from reality is itself nothing other than the precipitate of history in concepts."[7] Once again, exactly what Adorno intends is subtle, perhaps too subtle. For us, we hold that if even when one refuses to occupy the problem space of "History," capital H, and its master narratives of progress, decline, or stasis, nonetheless a thinker has still to deal in one manner or another with historicity. Historical factors are relevant for their contribution to an understanding of context, during the design, practice, and evaluation of inquiry.

In a contemporary mode, historical factors may well contribute to a narrative in many different ways (who were the Red Army Faction? When was the major wave of South Asian migration to Britain?). It is the historicity of the *Nachleben*, the catalyzing agents or eroding ones lurking out of the reach of our hardworking colleagues scouring and sorting the archives, that are part of the situation. The brittle striations equally can escape the attention of the genealogist who, at least in its classic form, seeks to show the contingency of the present by driving lines back into the past and showing or imagining their reassemblages, dissolutions, and forged molding into apparatuses.

Our efforts at narration are saturated by long years of conceptual work. Or, perhaps one could interpret Adorno's "precipitate" in its triple sense of something that hurries things along and the sudden acceleration of a process as well as what is distilled from a reaction.

Regardless—and enough discursive parrying with analogies of things past—for us "the precipitate of history in concepts" can refer to interpretations of the actual through cases that establish a certain distance and a certain relationship with those tacking between philosophy and anthropology. The distance is conceptual insofar as one is committed to a mode of narration that derives from the conceptual work of inquiry and its propositions and determinations but checks the drive to move backward into that mode of veridiction and its correlate mode of subjectivation. The relationship is a conceptual one to the degree that the *Nachleben, kairos,* and *Pathosformel* are themselves graspable through the precipitate of history in concepts and the anthropological practice of observing the patient giving of form by and for those testing, checking, and sounding the slim, yet seemingly available, passageways of freedom, however brittle the ground on which this work proceeds may be.

TERMS OF ENGAGEMENT

This repertoire of terms derives from the collaborative work, inquiry, and friendship of Anthony Stavrianakis, Gaymon Bennett, and Paul Rabinow over the course of roughly a decade. While building on a series of Rabinow's prior publications, it has coalesced during the process of collaborative participant-observation and the subsequent publication of four books: *The Accompaniment: Assembling the Contemporary* (Rabinow 2011); *Designing Human Practices: An Experiment with Synthetic Biology* (Bennett & Rabinow 2012); *Demands of the Day: On the Logic of Anthropological Inquiry* (Rabinow and Stavrianakis 2013); *Designs on the Contemporary: Anthropological Tests* (Rabinow and Stavrianakis 2014). Each of these books is published by the University of Chicago Press and it is fair to say that T. David Brent, and his assistant Priya Nelson, have provided care and encouragement throughout.

This repertoire, while not exhaustive, nonetheless provides the core configuration of terms that we have used, invented and/or modified to further our work.

D: Definition

U: Usage

actual

D: For John Dewey, thinking is an active response to a situation in which the everyday and taken-for-granted—the present—is troubled or breaking down.[1] The actual entails conceptual clarification and reduction into warrantable objects out of the swarming confusion of the present. The initial objective of inquiry is to transform the present into the actual. The products of inquiry into the present are the actual.

U: In this manner, once anthropology understands itself as starting with an already engaged activity, its task becomes one of participant-observation. The anthropologist must devise ways to focus on problems encountered and the challenge of qualifying them, analyzing them, and, if possible, remedying them. Consequently, anthropology is a situated practice; it begins in a contextualized present and moves conceptually and existentially toward the production of a transformed state of affairs, the actual.

agōn

D: Greek: "Contest; struggle."[2]

U: Deleuze and Guattari in *What Is Philosophy?* identify three terms as conditions for the emergence of philosophy in ancient Greece: *agōn*, venue, and *philia*.[3] The term stands between "communication" and "strife." It is a mode of engagement that is neither polemical nor rhetorical. It is a contest between friends seeking better understanding and better character.

anthrōpos

D: Greek: (The) human (being), generically and of individuals. Modern figures of *anthrōpos* have included the following: man, person, human kind, humans, and humanity.[4]

U: Throughout Western history *anthrōpos* has been a problem because of the heterogeneity of discourses that have been produced about what it is and the practices that constitute it. It has been given form in modernity as a figuration of life, labor, and language. The task of an anthropology of the contemporary is to identify sites of reproblematization. Prominent among such sites are developments connected to postgenomic biology.

askēsis

D: Greek: "Exercise, practice, training."[5]

U: A type of this worldly asceticism, which prepares the subject for access to truth. "An exercise of oneself in the activity of thought."[6] *Askēsis* is composed of diverse practices—examination of activities, control of representations, tests of thought—all aiming toward a *technē tou biou* and the avoidance of *stultitia*.

In modernity, these practices have been marginalized as access to the truth has been made to turn on method. Inquiry into the contemporary requires a reinvention and reintroduction of ascetic practices.

ataraxia

D: Greek: "Impassiveness, coolness, calmness."[7] A key Stoic virtue: the absence of inner turmoil and the capacity of a subject to control its thoughts, actions, and passions, such that the subject is undisturbed by unexpected, fortunate or unfortunate events.

U: Older virtues such as *ataraxia* must be reproblematized and rethought for the contemporary. The truth claims underlying and justifying these older virtues were based on a cosmos. Practice in inquiry today requires a replacement term turning on a different point of reference.

Ausgang

D: German: "Exit." "Kant defines *Aufklärung* [enlightenment] in an almost entirely negative way, as an *Ausgang,* an 'exit,' a 'way out.'"[8]

U: Within an anthropological practice *Ausgang* serves as a concept to pose two interconnected problems: (1) how to leave the inquiry; and (2) what comes after the participant-observation stage of inquiry?

Betrachtung (-en)

D: German: "Contemplation; examination; observation." For Nietzsche, *Betrachtung* entails a stance (*Haltung*) or mood of life (Ger. *Lebenstimmung*) that includes theoretical understanding, sensory perception and a drive or a force.[9] The English translation "observations," or French *considerations,* misses the refractory intent of an engaged and active state. Hence, *Betrachtungen* is better conveyed as something more like the purposely oxymoronic "vigorous contemplations."[10]

U: *Betrachtung* as a concept is part of a practice of inquiry that Niklas Luhmann called "second-order observation" (*Beobachtung zweiter Ordnung*). Second-order observation aims to clarify habits and dispositions by opening up the question of what might need to be changed or maintained on the part of those observed. It does this through a combination of observation and intervention. Such observation and intervention, as dispassionate as it may be, is likely to provoke a reaction. This reaction, at least initially, oscillates between the poles of indifference and violence.[11]

bios

D: Greek: "Life, not animal life (*zoē*), but mode of life, manner of living of human beings."[12]

U: The term *bios* used in a contemporary sense refers to a domain of anthropological problematization after the foundational terms of nature and culture have been relativized.

case

D: Following in the tradition of casuistry in its various ramifications from ethics to law and medicine, cases are distinguished from examples. Whereas examples function to illustrate theory, cases are singular while also having ramifying analogical relations to other cases.

U: The significance of a case turns neither on its singularity nor on its universality. Rather, it turns on a productive relation between the necessity of taking into account the particularity of a given case as well as the relevant metric that specified that case and directs inquiry to pursue a series of analogical cases. A particular challenge for anthropology is that, unlike in law and medicine, there are relatively few settled and uncontested forms, venues, and standards of judgment by way of which and through which what counts as a case can be taken for granted.

collaboration

D: As a mode of work collaboration should be distinguished from cooperation. Collaboration, unlike cooperation, entails common definition of problems and shared practices of addressing those problems albeit with coordinated use of different skill sets and experiences. A cooperative mode consists in demarcated work on a common problem with regular exchange.

U: A collaborative mode proceeds from an interdependent division of labor on shared problems. In a contemporary mode, collaboration is both an object of inquiry and a mode of engagement. Such a mode is often resisted in the name of the sufficiency of existing expertise, thereby blocking the design of new forms of inquiry.

contemporary

D: An assemblage of both old and new elements and their interactions and interfaces. The contemporary has two senses: to exist at the same time as something else and to carry a distinctive style. The first meaning has temporal but no historical connotations. The second sense has both: just as "the modern" can be thought of as a moving ratio of tradition and modernity, so the contemporary "is a moving ratio of modernity, moving through the recent past and near future in a (non-linear) space."[13]

U: As a temporal and ontological problem space, the contemporary is both an object and objective of anthropology. Inquiry into the contemporary is both analytic and synthetic. It is analytic in that sets of relations must be decomposed and specified, synthetic in that these relations must be recomposed and given new form. In this sense, work on the contemporary falls within a zone of analytic consideration in that it consists of linking the recent past to the near future and the near future to the recent past.

design

D: In thinking about the equipment and practices needed for an anthropology of the contemporary, a focus on the problem of design highlights the need to consider both upstream and downstream parameters. Upstream: capable of integrating heterogeneous elements according to a particular metric. Downstream: capable of functioning in specific cases while remaining available for rearticulation in other cases.

U: *The Accompaniment* (2011), *Designing Human Practices* (2012), *Demands of the Day* (2013), and *Designs on the Contemporary* (2014) present cases of design. Each highlights the collaborative and experimental character of contemporary practice. It builds in reiterative and remediative options as the inquiry ramifies.

discordancy

D: Following John Dewey, thinking is a response to types of breakdown in practice which lead to discomfort and discordancy.[14]

U: Attention to discordancy links inquiry and ethics. Discordancy is a question of ethics insofar as rectification of discordant situations requires recursive discernment of ethical practices set within defined modes of jurisdiction. By working through cases, abstract philosophic debates are eschewed and replaced by the invention of equipment and practices. Such attention to discordancy facilitates the evaluation of the limits to the growth of capacities imposed by specific situations.

durcharbeiten

D: Freud used the term *durcharbeiten*, or "working through," to capture the processual and temporal dimension of the sporadic release of blocked emotion. Jean Starobinksi shows that before Freud the term *durcharbeiten* was already a perfectly acceptable German word. In *Elective Affinities*, Goethe describes how Charlotte, the heroine, quietly withdraws from the public scene in order to evaluate her acts and feelings through the silent work of self-reflection.

U: *Durcharbeiten* can be a quiet affair, one that requires time, demands reflection as well as affect, and works through the production of a form of narration. Further, the production of that form of narration requires more than one participant: analyst and analyzed in a psychoanalytic setting, author and reader in a literary one. An anthropological *durcharbeiten* involves working over the discordancies and indeterminations of participant-observation. This facilitates movement toward subsequent modal states of thinking.

equipment / *paraskeuē*

D: Greek: "Equipment or preparedness."[15] Equipment, though conceptual in design and formulation, is pragmatic in use. Defined abstractly, equipment is a set of truth claims, affects and ethical orientations designed and composed into a practice.[16]

U: Equipment, which has historically taken different forms, enables practical responses to changing conditions brought about by specific problems, events, and general reconfigurations. Composed in a contemporary mode, equipment takes different forms. This variability stems from the fact that the contemporary is neither a unified epoch nor a culture and consequently there is no reason to expect there would be a single form of equipment.

ethical substance

D: "The way in which the individual has to constitute this or that part of himself as the prime material of his moral conduct."[17]

U: A contemporary problem, to which the issue of ethical substance is central, is how to conduct projects in collaborative participant-observation, among anthropologists and bioscientists, that seek to identify and bring together truth and conduct, with particular attention to collaboration and *parastēma*. Such endeavors are likely to encounter negligence, indifference, and active blockage, requiring their pursuit in appropriate venues with appropriate equipment.

ethos

D: Greek: The manners and habits of *anthrōpos*, including dispositions and character.

U: The term carries with it the double sense of what came to be called the cultural with an emphasis on mood as well as the ethical as a mode of subjectivation. How to transform a modern ethos into a contemporary one constitutes a core challenge for *anthrōpos* today.

eudaemonia

D: Greek: The condition of being well; flourishing.

U: Used as a central term in steering (in the Platonic sense) the practice of participant-observation during fieldwork and the work which follows. As a metric, flourishing enables the posing of questions outside instrumental rationality, which dominate both the bio- and social sciences. A fundamental distinction between prosperity, amelioration, and flourishing reintroduces the challenge of the worth of inquiry and its products.

form/Form-giving

D: The composition of something in the world. The power of form for inquiry is that it tunes attention to the question of historical ontology: who are we as beings and how we exist in the world.

U: The challenge of form-giving is to determine, bring together, and compose relevant elements in such a way that care and thought might become both a practice and an outcome. Thus the labor of form-giving constitutes the ethical challenge of inquiry.[18]

foyer d'expérience

D: French: Foucault identifies *foyers d'expérience* as venues in which "forms of a possible knowledge (*savoir*), normative frameworks of behavior for individuals, and potential modes of existence for possible subjects are linked together."[19]

U: An anthropology of the contemporary pays close attention to such venues so as to ask how configurations of veridiction, jurisdiction, and subjectivation are breaking down and being repaired (*sōzein*).

Gemüt

D: German: "Disposition."

Kant in his *Anthropology from a Pragmatic Point of View* asks how questions of "can" and "should" can be given a relation in the self-understanding of *anthrōpos*. Kant has a cosmopolitical aim in answering this question: knowledge of *anthrōpos* as a citizen of the world. In his *Introduction to Kant's Anthropology* Foucault underscores that although the *Anthropology* has a cosmopolitical aim, in fact it takes up *anthrōpos* as an object from the interior point of view of the *Gemüt*, the site of self-affectation of the human being.

Foucault shows how Kant's critical philosophical project stems from his anthropological project: the problematic play of the animating principle of the work of ideas (*Geist*) on the field of experience and self-affectation (*Gemüt*).

U: *Gemüt* has proved to be important as the locus of equipmental attention, so as to open the possibility of a pragmatic reduction of possible ideas, values and forms. One specific set of forms in which equipmental attention can be given to the *Gemüt* is narrative mood.

Haltung (-en)

D: German: "Posture, stance, style, manner, attitude, composure." *Haltung* makes visible the significance of a specific occasion, or turning point, which is much more than mere timing (*kairos*). The term was turned into a concept and practice by Bertold Brecht as a means of changing the role of the actor in the theater.[20]

U: In the practical, conceptual, and affective work of leaving the field, *Haltung* is the concept around which the anthropologist can develop a manner as well as a tempo and timing of exiting or *Ausgang*. It underlines not only the conceptual work of the subject in anthropology but also the affective and corporeal labor required to carry through participant-observation.

horos (-oi)

D: Greek: "A limit, rule, standard, measure; in mathematics, *horoi* are the terms of a ratio or proportion."[21] In book 6 of the *Nicomachean Ethics*, Aristotle writes that one of the objects of ethics is the choice of standard determining the manner of undertaking an activity.[22]

U: For Aristotle, to know about virtue, it is not enough to simply define a mean. Rather it is necessary to know by what standard a mean becomes a practice. The fact that Aristotle never actually names this standard (*horos*) has left Western philosophy with the problem of the unresolved relations among and between thinking, *bios* and *eudaemonia*. Those engaged in inquiry are confronted explicitly or implicitly with bringing these terms into a common form.

indeterminacy

D: Indeterminacy is one type of breakdown that occasions thinking.[23] Following Dewey it is a type of problem (as opposed to discordancy) occasioned by breakdowns of signification, meaning, and coherence.

U: Moving through inquiry from greater to lesser indeterminacy requires recursive experimentation with various defined modes of veridiction. Inquiry into indeterminacy requires the labor of the diagnosis of problems and conceptual clarification leading to warranted propositions.

kairos

D: Greek: "Of time, in or at the right time, in season, seasonable, timely, opportune."[24] *Kairos* is the seizing of a significant turning point by the subject that can later be characterized as an event. *Kairos* carries with it a sense of significant alteration of motion and the opening up or closing down of multiple possibilities.

U: Turning points or ruptures can be conceptualized and narrated as a series, such as "instance," "episode," "event." The ancient Greeks called a *kairos* the recognition and capability of acting at the right moment, in the right manner. Anthropologists working in a contemporary mode must be attentive to differentiating turning points after a breakdown or an indetermination is diagnosed. By so doing the significance of a turning point can be conceptualized and narrated as a *kairos*.

lēpsis

D: Greek: "A taking hold, seizing, catching; an accepting, receiving, getting."[25]

U: The root *lēpsis* names a contemporary search for narrative forms which capture both the active and passive aspects of the anthropological task of working over an experience. Two forms of *lēpsis*, *metalēpsis* and *syndialēpsis*, have proven relevant.

metalēpsis

D: Greek: "Participation, communion; a taking up, alternation; a taking one thing instead of another; the use of one word for another."[26] Harold Bloom has characterized *metalēpsis* as a trope-reversing trope, which substitutes one word for another in prior rhetorical figures.[27]

U: *Metalēpsis* can be used as a narrative form in which breakdowns in the past and present can be worked through and worked over by way of a future projection, substitution, and a hoped-for identification.

metric

D: The standard by which aspects of things are selected and coordinated in a relational field.[28]

U: Diagnostically, three metrics—prosperity, amelioration, and flourishing (*eudaemonia*)—have proven central to the current reproblematization of truth and ethics.

mode of jurisdiction

D: A mode of jurisdiction distinguishes normative frameworks of behavior for individuals and functions as the basis for governance.[29]

U: During inquiry, attention must be paid to normative frameworks, which operate as objects of study as well as constraints on participant-observation. Those seeking to remediate modes of jurisdiction must take into account their deep embeddedness in unequal power relations. Introducing a discussion of such embeddedness tends to activate and reinscribe these inequalities rather than increase capacities.

mode of subjectivation

D: A mode of subjectivation designates the manner in which possible forms of existence for a subject can be realized. The range of possibilities depends on existing modes of jurisdiction as well as the ethical practices undertaken in view of those existing modes.

U: An anthropology of the contemporary seeks through inquiry to identify the state of such determinations as well as the opportunities potentially available. In this way modes of subjectivation function both as objects and objectives of inquiry and judgment.

mode of veridiction

D: A mode of veridiction distinguishes the manner in which speech acts are produced and made to count in a historical register of true and false.

U: Veridictional practices are always related to jurisdictional and ethical modes. The stakes of *anthrōpos* turn on bringing the situation of *logos* to light within these other determinations.

mood

D: "Name given to different forms of the verb that are used to affirm more or less the same thing in question and to express . . . the different points of view from which the life or the action is looked at."[30]

U: Two moods dominate academic discourse today: irony and tragedy. Two other moods—pathos and comedy—prove fertile to enlarge the possibilities of understanding and practice in a contemporary ethos.

Nachleben

D: German: "Afterlife or survival." Aby Warburg gave the term a specific meaning by using it conceptually to capture the sense of present but not thematized stylized motifs such as certain gestures that he found enduring from ancient Greece friezes through Botticelli's paintings.

U: In inquiry, *Nachleben* refers to those objects, affects, and motions in modernity which are excluded or escape from modernist forms but nonetheless exist in the present. Identifying the presence of *Nachleben* in a situation contributes to the articulation of a contemporary mode. This practice foregrounds the challenge of bringing elements of the old and the new into a distinctive form thereby enhancing understanding and freeing one from constraints wrongly taken to be determinative.

parastēma (-ta)

D: *Parastēma* is a character term. It refers to a subject's relation to the interconnection of truth and conduct. Ordinarily referring to the stature of a character, or else of the bearing and poise of a subject, it is not simply a mark of civilized manners, which could be understood as behavior arbitrated by a rule. Rather, *parastēmata* are what Foucault has called an "ethical substance"—that which must be the object of conscious consideration—the questions a person must keep in mind in order to do what they do truthfully. *Parastēmata* are thus principles or maxims.

U: In our use, the concept of *parastēma* indexes neither a principle nor a behavior learned, but rather the need to make a judgment about the distance or proximity between claims to truth (warranted assertibility) and the conduct of life (*bios*).

Pathosformel

D: German: Literally, "forms given to pathos." The term was turned into a concept by the art historian Aby Warburg in his work on the history of style. It has a double sense: the attempt to give form to situations or moods of pathos and the only partial success of such attempts.

U: Recognizing both the hybrid referent and concept, the term can play a powerful role in directing anthropological inquiry as well as decisions about an appropriate form of narration. Hence, deploying the term encompasses propositional, judgmental, and narratival registers. The practice of form-giving under the sign of pathos (as object and mood) contrasts with those of irony, comedy, and tragedy.

parrhēsia

D: Greek: "Outspokenness; frankness."[31] A mode of veridiction which has three characteristics: it binds the speaker to the truth of that which is said (i.e., the speaker must truly think what is said is true); it entails a danger to the truth-speaking subject; and the ramifications of what is spoken cannot be known in advance.[32]

U: By practicing *parrhēsia*, the truth is made actual. Speaking truth claims in this mode not only allows for the possibility of unforeseen ramifications, but more importantly, increases one's capacity and disposition to speak the truth in consequential situations. This practice is thus scientifically and ethically essential to anthropology.[33]

philia

D: Greek: "Affectionate regard, friendship, usually between equals."[34]

U: Deleuze and Guattari identify three terms as conditions for the emergence of philosophy in ancient Greece: *agōn*, venue, and *philia*. Aristotle, for example, in book 8 of the *Ethics*, places great emphasis on the foundational place of friendship and its forms for philosophy as part of a flourishing existence (*eudaemonia*). The challenge today is to reproblematize the terms of philosophic friendship in an anthropological mode.

problem

D: A problem is composed of conceptual and practical poles. On the conceptual side a problem invites the work of transforming breakdowns, indeterminacy, discordancy, etc., into material (questions, objects, sites of inquiry, etc.) for thought. On the practical side a problem invites the formulation, design, and facilitation of possible courses of action that have been opened up and made available as solutions.

U: The relations among and between inquiry, equipment, venue, and collaboration only take their form in relation to specific problems. Their form is not pregiven nor fixed such that it can be methodologically applied to instances arrayed as examples.

sōzein

D: Greek: To save, especially from a threatening danger; to protect or guard; preservation of virtue; to defend; to keep in a certain proper state. In its richest sense, *sōzein* refers to that which is a source of good.[35]

U: In anthropological practice the term plays a role in the senses of repairing, protecting, and defending the worth of inquiry and those engaged in it. The concept opens up a space of affect in which attention can be legitimately devoted to addressing or confronting a range of breakdowns as part of the scientific life.

stultitia

D: Latin: "Foolishness, folly."[36] Seneca uses the term to indicate a state of being in which the subject is fragmented and unsettled. For Seneca the *stultus* is someone who has not cared for himself, is blown by the wind and too open to the external world. The *stultus* indiscriminately lets in representations from the outside world.[37]

U: Those engaged in inquiry and thinking are often haunted by *stultitia*. Hence, recognizing the affects and effects of *stultitia* can aid them in their practice.

syndialēpsis

D: Greek: The doing or undertaking of scientific and intellectual research, together with others.

U: This archaic term, used neologistically, surprisingly captures the critical dimension of a collaborative and vindicatory *lēpsis* (i.e., the work requisite to move through the actual to the contemporary).

technē

D: Greek: "Art, skill, craft; way, manner or means by which a thing is gained; a set of rules, system or method of making or doing."[38]

U: *Technē* is an essential component of form-giving in veridictional and jurisdictional, as well as subjectivational, practices. Attention to *technē* in the conduct of anthropological and philosophic work confronts the challenge of turning universals into philosophic and anthropological problems which can be inquired into and reflected upon. *Technē* is thus an essential mediator but not a telos.

technē tou biou

D: Greek: The art of ordering life; producing, in its critical dimension, a worthwhile manner of living.

U: *Technē tou biou* is both what one attends to anthropologically in the world as well as what one must attend to in order to conduct anthropological work. Given the argument that the foundational functions of nature and culture, as well as history, have been eclipsed, attention to *technē tou biou* is required to understand the interconnected ethical and veridicational stakes of work on the contemporary.

venues

D: The scene, site, or setting in which specialists design and synthesize activity.[39]

U: The invention of venues is necessary for the facilitation of collaborative anthropological practice. In that way they equally become significant objects of anthropological attention and practice.

vindicare

D: Latin: Vindication; laying claim to a thing; a taking into protection, a defense.[40]

U: Vindication is opposed to self-justification. It is the product of long work on the self and others as well as veridictional testing. Once achieved it contributes to an affect of care and well-being, even under conflictual circumstances, as well as a stance of assuredness in the claims arising from an inquiry.

warranted assertibility

D: Propositions attained through inquiry in an anthropological sense. John Dewey writes: "All knowledge, or warranted assertion, depends upon inquiry." Inquiry turns on only what is questionable (and questioned). It always involves a skeptical element, or what Peirce called "fallibilism."[41]

U: The "truth game" of anthropology is inescapably connected to pragmatic inquiry. The tested results of a series of experiments and rectifications might be called "propositions," and these are what can be warranted as the products of one stage of inquiry. As warranted, these products can be taken up as objects which can be reproblematized in the disciplined pursuit of further and more specifically defined objectives. Inquiry and the warranted assertions it produces, in the pragmatist tradition, form an integral part of an ongoing form of life.

NOTES

PREFACE

1. Paul Rabinow, *Marking Time: On the Anthropology of the Contemporary* (Princeton, NJ: Princeton University Press, 2007), 2.
2. Paul Rabinow, *Anthropos Today: Reflections on Modern Equipment* (Princeton, NJ: Princeton University Press, 2003); *Marking Time; The Accompaniment: Assembling the Contemporary* (Chicago: University of Chicago Press, 2011).
3. Paul Rabinow and Anthony Stavrianakis, *Demands of the Day: On the Logic of Anthropological Inquiry* (Chicago: University of Chicago Press, 2013).
4. Michel Foucault, *Le Gouvernement de soi et des autres, Cours au Collège de France, 1982–83* (Paris: Seuil, 2008), 4–5.
5. Gilles Deleuze, *Foucault* (Paris: Éditions de Minuit, 2004), 55.
6. Rabinow, *Marking Time*, 101–128.

PART ONE: INTRODUCTION

1. Michel Foucault, *Introduction to Kant's Anthropology*, trans. Kate Briggs and Robert Nigro (Los Angeles: Semiotext(e), 2008), 63.
2. Immanuel Kant, *Lectures on Anthropology*, trans. Robert B. Louden et al. (Cambridge: Cambridge University Press, 2013).
3. Michel Foucault, *Qu'est-ce que les lumières?*, in *Dits et écrits*, vol. 2, *1976—1988* (Paris: Gallimard, 2001), 1381–97; "What Is Enlightenment?," in *The Foucault Reader*, ed. Paul Rabinow (New York: Pantheon, 1984), 32–50.
4. Immanuel Kant and Michel Foucault, *Anthropologie du point de vue pragmatique et introduction à l'anthropologie* (Paris: Vrin, 2008).
5. Sardinha Diogo, "De livres considérés à tort comme mineurs," *Rue Descartes*, no. 75 (2012–2013): 1–5.
6. Foucault, *Qu'est-ce que les lumières?*
7. Marc Djaballah, *Kant, Foucault, and Forms of Experience* (New York: Routledge, 2011), 174–84.
8. Immanuel Kant, *Anthropology from a Pragmatic Point of View* (Cambridge: Cambridge University Press, 2006), 3.
9. Foucault, *Introduction to Kant's Anthropology*, 51.
10. Howard Caygill, *A Kant Dictionary* (Oxford: John Wiley & Sons, 1995), 210.
11. Kant, *Anthropology*, 120.

12. Foucault, *Introduction to Kant's Anthropology*, 63.
13. Gilles Deleuze, *Kant's Critical Philosophy: The Doctrine of the Faculties* (London: Athlone, 1984), 8.
14. Kant, *Anthropology*, 3.
15. Jörg Volbers, "Michel Foucault, philosophe de la liberté? Sur sa lecture de Kant dans l'introduction à l'anthropologie," *Rue Descartes*, no. 75 (2012–2013): 11.
16. Foucault, *Introduction to Kant's Anthropology*, 33.
17. Ibid.
18. Immanuel Kant, "Idea for a Universal History with a Cosmopolitan Aim," trans. Allen W. Wood, in *Anthropology, History, and Education*, trans. Robert B. Louden and Günter Zöller (Cambridge: Cambridge University Press, 2008).
19. Bruno Latour, "An Attempt at a Compositionist Manifesto," *New Literary History* 41, no. 3 (Summer 2010): 478.

CHAPTER ONE
1. Foucault, *Introduction to Kant's Anthropology*, 65.
2. Foucault, "What Is Enlightenment?," 50.
3. John Dewey, "Propositions, Warranted Assertibility, and Truth, " *Journal of Philosophy* 38, no. 7 (1941): 169–86.
4. On the notion of "experimental system" see Hans-Jorg Rheinberger, *Towards a History of Epistemic Things: Synthesizing Proteins in the Test Tube* (Palo Alto, CA: Stanford University Press, 1997).
5. Paul Rabinow and Gaymon Bennett, *Designing Human Practices: An Experiment with Synthetic Biology* (Chicago: Chicago University Press, 2012).
6. See chap. 2 for a technical discussion.
7. Giorgio Agamben, *Homo Sacer: Sovereign Power and Bare Life* (Palo Alto, CA: Stanford University Press, 1998).
8. Nikolas Rose, *The Politics of Life Itself: Biomedicine, Power, and Subjectivity in the Twenty-First Century* (Princeton: Princeton University Press, 2006).
9. On "world view" and "perspective" as key elements of modernity, see Martin Heidegger, "The Age of the World Picture," in *Heidegger: Off the Beaten Track*, trans. and ed. Julian Young and Kenneth Haynes (Cambridge: Cambridge University Press, 2002).
10. Hans Blumenberg, " 'Imitation of Nature': Toward a Prehistory of the Idea of the Creative Being," *Qui Parle* 12, no. 1 (Spring/Summer 2000): 17–54.
11. Hans Blumenberg, *Paradigms for a Metaphorology* (Ithaca, NY: Cornell University Press, 2010).
12. Robert M. Wallace, "Introduction," in *The Legitimacy of the Modern Age*, by Hans Blumenberg, trans. and ed. Robert M. Wallace (Cambridge, MA: MIT Press, 1985), xv.
13. Ibid.
14. Ibid.
15. Ibid, xvii–xviii.
16. Ibid, xviii.
17. Ibid.
18. Blumenberg, *Legitimacy of the Modern Age*, 138.
19. Wallace, "Introduction," xxi.
20. Blumenberg, "Imitation of Nature," 46.
21. Ibid.
22. Ibid.

23. Clifford Geertz, "Thinking as a Moral Act: Ethical Dimensions of Anthropological Fieldwork in the New States," in *Antioch Review* 28, no. 2 (1968): 140.

24. Rabinow et al, *Designs for an Anthropology of the Contemporary* (Durham, NC: Duke University Press, 2008), 16.

25. Geertz, "Thinking as a Moral Act," 146.

26. Ibid.

27. Rabinow and Bennett, *Designing Human Practices*, 7.

28. Clifford Geertz, "Ideology as a Cultural System," in *The Interpretation of Cultures* (New York: Basic Books, 1973), 204.

29. Ibid., 211.

30. Ibid., 212.

31. Ibid.

32. Geertz, "Thinking as Moral Act," 154.

33. Ibid.

34. Geertz, "Ideology as a Cultural System," 230.

35. Ibid., 231.

36. Paul Rabinow, "Humanism as Nihilism: The Bracketing of Truth and Seriousness in American Cultural Anthropology," in *Social Science as Moral Inquiry*, ed. N. Haan et al., 52–75 (New York: Columbia University Press), reprinted in *The Accompaniment* (Chicago: University of Chicago Press, 2011).

37. See Clifford Geertz, "The Impact of the Concept of Culture on the Concept of Man," in *Interpretation of Cultures*, 33–54.

38. Godfrey Lienhardt, "Modes of Thought in Primitive Society," *New Blackfriars* 34, no. 399 (June 1953): 269–77; Talal Asad, "The Concept of Cultural Translation in British Social Anthropology," in *Writing Culture: The Poetics and Politics of Ethnography*, ed. James Clifford and George E. Marcus (Berkeley: University of California Press, 1986).

39. Cf. Theodor W. Adorno, *The Positivist Dispute in German Sociology* (London: Heinemann, 1976).

40. Norma Haan et al., eds., *Social Science as Moral Inquiry* (New York: Columbia University Press, 1983), 6.

41. See Bourdieu's critique of intellecutlist theory in *Outline of a Theory of Practice* (Cambridge University Press 1977), 97–109.

42. James Clifford, "Introduction: Partial Truth," in *Writing Culture*, 18.

43. Robert Bellah et al., *Habits of the Heart: Individualism and Commitment in American Life* (Berkeley: University of California Press, 1985).

44. George E. Marcus and Michael M. J. Fischer, *Anthropology as Cultural Critique: An Experimental Moment in the Human Sciences* (Chicago: University of Chicago Press, 1986); Aihwa Ong and Stephen J. Collier, *Global Assemblages: Technology, Politics, and Ethics as Anthropological Problems* (Oxford: Wiley, 2004).

45. Rabinow and Stavrianakis, *Demands of the Day*.

46. Michel Foucault, *The Hermeneutics of the Subject: Lectures at the Collège de France 1981–1982* (New York: Palgrave Macmillan, 2005); *The Government of Self and Others: Lectures at the College de France, 1982–1983* (New York: Palgrave Macmillan, 2010); *The Courage of Truth: The Government of Self and Others II; Lectures at the Collège de France, 1983–1984* (New York: Palgrave Macmillan, 2011).

47. Michel Foucault, "Omnes et singulatim: Towards a Critique of Political Reason," in *Power: Essential Works of Foucault: 1954–1984*, ed. James D. Faubion, 298–325 (New York: New Press, 2000).

48. Michel Foucault, "On the Genealogy of Ethics: Overview of Work in Progress," in *The Foucault Reader*, ed. Paul Rabinow (New York: Pantheon, 1984), 340–72.

49. Foucault, *Hermeneutics of the Subject*, 178.

50. Ibid., 18.

51. Ibid., 19.

52. Paul Rabinow, *Anthropos Today*, 4.

CHAPTER TWO

1. Tom Burke, *Dewey's New Logic: A Reply to Russell* (Chicago: University of Chicago Press, 1994), 238.

2. Rabinow, *Anthropos Today*, 7; Paul Rabinow, Andrew Lakoff, and Stephen Collier, "Biosecurity: Towards an anthropology of the contemporary," *Anthropology Today* 20, no. 5 (October 2004): 3–7; Paul Rabinow, "How to Submit to Inquiry: Dewey and Foucault," *Pluralist* 7, no. 3 (2012): 36.

3. Tom Burke, *Dewey's New Logic*, 22.

4. Ibid., 23.

5. Rabinow and Stavrianakis, *Demands of the Day*, 8–10.

6. John Dewey, *Essays in Experimental Logic* (Chicago: University of Chicago Press, 1916; rep. New York: Dover, 2004).

7. Rabinow and Stavrianakis, *Demands of the Day*.

8. On *parastēma*, which should be understood to encompass a range of terms such as "poise"; "stature" and in the plural, "principles or maxims," see Foucault, *Hermeneutics of the Subject*, 291.

9. For more detail see the working through of our logic of inquiry in Rabinow and Stavrianakis, *Demands of the Day*, 33.

10. Burke, *Dewey's New Logic*, 148–49.

11. Ibid., 149.

12. Ibid., 205.

13. Ibid., 206. See John Dewey, "Propositions, Warranted Assertibility, and Truth," *Journal of Philosophy* 38, no. 7 (1941): 175.

14. Ibid., 179.

15. Ibid., 149.

16. Ibid., 155.

17. Translation by James Ker, *The Deaths of Seneca* (Oxford: Oxford University Press, 2009), 156.

18. John Dewey, *Logic: The Theory of Inquiry* (New York: Henry Holt, 1938), 13.

19. Rabinow and Stavrianakis, *Demands of the Day*, 91.

20. Foucault, *Hermeneutics of the Subject*, 9

21. James Ker, *Nocturnal Letters: Roman Temporal Practices and Seneca's Epistulae Morales*, diss., University of California–Berkeley, 2002, 1.

22. Foucault, *The Hermeneutics of the Subject*, 212.

23. Ibid.

24. Ibid., 271.

25. Seneca, "On the Tranquility of Mind," in *Dialogues and Essays*, trans. John Davie (Oxford: Oxford University Press, 2009), 113.

26. Ibid., 116.

27. Ibid., 118.

28. Foucault, *Hermeneutics of the Subject*.

CHAPTER THREE

1. Michel Foucault, "Pierre Boulez, l'écran traversé" (1982), *Dits et écrits*, "On croit volontiers qu'une culture s'attache plus à ses valeurs que à ses formes, que celles-ci, facilement, peuvent être modifiée, abandonnés, reprises; que seul le sens enracine profondément. C'est méconnaitre combien les formes, quand elles se défont ou se naissent, ont pu provoquer d'étonnement ou susciter de haine; c'est méconnaitre qu'on tient plus aux manières de voir, de dire, de faire et de pensée qu'à ce qu'on voit, qu'à ce qu'on pense, dit ou fait. Le combat de formes en Occident a été aussi acharné, sinon plus, que celui des idées ou des valeurs" (219–20).

2. Gilles Deleuze and Felix Guattari, *What Is Philosophy?* (New York: Columbia University Press, 1996), 10.

3. Deleuze and Guattari, *What Is Philosophy?*, 9.

4. *Ibid*, 12.

5. Foucault alludes in his commentary to serial music and its ramifications with a strangely repetitive demurral as to his own incomprehension of Boulez's music at the time; this distancing is striking since Foucault himself had been a close observer of the contemporary music scene along with his partner of an earlier time, the composer Jean Barraqué.

6. Foucault, "Pierre Boulez, l'écran traversé" (1982), *Dits et Ecrits*, "C'est méconnaitre qu'on tient plus aux manières de voir, de dire, de faire et de pensée qu'à ce qu'on voit, qu'à ce qu'on pense, dit ou fait" (220).

7. Foucault, "Pierre Boulez, l'écran traversé": "Ont pris une allure singulière; c'est le 'formel' lui-même, c'est le travail réfléchi sur les systèmes de formes qui est devenu un enjeu. Et un remarquable objet d'hostilités morales, de débats esthétiques et d'affrontements politiques" (220).

8. In 1982, Foucault was already embarked on an inquiry into the problematization of the form of life of a contemporary philosopher. This embarkation, one might add, was at a moment when analytic philosophy and cognitive science with all their formalisms were ascendant in France.

9. Paul Rabinow and Gaymon Bennett, "A Diagnostic of Equipmental Platforms," *ARC Working Paper*, no. 9 (2007).

10. Ibid.

11. After inquiry, we understood that we were dealing with a proposition and that it had been disconfirmed.

    In 2011, we knew that the object was not a figure and was not *anthrōpos*, but rather actual configurations of discordancy and configurations of the actual. We could confirm this. Then the challenge became to move from propositions to judgments. Such a move would be illegitimate if one skipped this step and moved straight to judgments.

12. Cf. Paul Rabinow, "Why There Is No Contemporary Bioscience, Only a Modern One," in *Accompaniment*.

13. Foucault, *Hermeneutics of the Subject*, 17.

14. We were surprised that this motion from the present to the actual, from the ethnographic to the anthropological, was apparently tacit at best within the current practices of the discipline. Just as fieldwork had become a topic of inquiry and writing, so to it seemed logical that after-fieldwork would become a topic of inquiry and writing. In that light, we wrote a book about the logic of anthropological inquiry, *Demands of the Day*.

15. George Long, trans., *Meditations of the Emperor Marcus Aurelius Antoninus* (London: Chesterfield Society, n.d.), bk. 3, p. 11: "For nothing is so productive of elevation of mind as to be able to examine methodically and truly every object which is presented to you in life, and always to look at things so as to see at the same time what kind of universe this is, and what kind of use everything performs in it, and what worth everything has with reference to the whole, and what with reference to man, who is a citizen of the highest city, of which all other cities are like families; what each thing is, and of what it is composed, and how long it is the nature of this thing to endure which now makes an impression on me, and what virtue I have need of with respect to it. . . . At the same time however in things indifferent I attempt to ascertain the worth of each."

16. Michel Foucault, "On the Genealogy of Ethics," in *Beyond Structuralism and Hermeneutics* (Chicago: University of Chicago Press, 1983); Paul Rabinow, "Introduction: The History of Systems of Thought," in *Essential Works of Foucault (1954–1984)*, Volume 1: *Ethics*, edited by Paul Rabinow (New York: New Press, 1994).

17. Paul Rabinow, "Introduction: The History of Systems of Thought," in *Essential Works of Foucault (1954–1984)*, vol. 1, *Ethics*, ed. Paul Rabinow (New York: New Press, 1994).

18. Aristotle, *Nicomachean Ethics*, trans., Harris Rackham (Cambridge: Loeb Classical Library, 1934).

19. Sandra Peterson asks, "What is the standard or criterion to which right reasoning looks?" As Peterson explains, there have been several responses to this question among Aristotle scholars: Some like Akrill think he has raised a question which he fails to answer; others like Rowe think he ultimately makes the point, by not answering explicitly the question of what this standard is, that there is an *horos* calibrated the question of a flourishing life, but it cannot be given in advance of cases and situations. We agree with all three in rejecting the idea that the *horos* could be contemplation.

20. Gilles Deleuze, *Nietzsche and Philosophy* (New York: Continuum, 1986), 2.

21. June Allison, *Power and Preparedness in Thucydides* (Baltimore, MD: Johns Hopkins University Press, 1989).

22. See James Faubion, *Modern Greek Lessons* (Princeton, NJ: Princeton University Press, 1995), 117.

23. Aurelius, *Meditations*, I.7.

PART TWO: INTRODUCTION

1. Foucault, *Hermeneutics of the Subject: Lectures at the Collège de France 1981–1982* (New York: Palgrave Macmillan, 2005), 466–67. Translation modified. "Que le monde, à travers le bios, soit devenu cette expérience à travers lequel nous nous connaissons nous-même, cet exercice à travers laquelle nous nous connaissons nous-mêmes, cet exercice à travers lequel nous nous nous transformons ou nous nous sauvons, je crois que cela, c'est une transformation, une mutation très importante par rapport à ce qu'était la pensée grecque classique, à savoir que le bios doit être l'objet d'une technē, c'est-à-dire d'un art raisonnable et rationnel."

2. Foucault, "What Is Enlightenment?," 39.

3. Max Weber, "'Objectivity' in Social Science and Social Policy," in Max Weber, *The Methodology of the Social Sciences*, trans. Edward Shils and Henry Finch (Glencoe, IL: Free Press, 1949), 93.

4. Max Weber, *The Protestant Ethic and the Spirit of Capitalism* (New York: Scribner, 1958), 182.

5. Weber, "'Objectivity' in Social Science and Social Policy," 68.
6. John Dewey, *Reconstruction in Philosophy*, enlarged edition (Boston: Beacon Press, 1948), xxvii.
7. Rabinow and Stavrianakis, *Demands of the Day*.
8. Foucault, *Hermeneutics of the Subject*, 182.
9. Henry George Liddell and Robert Scott, *A Greek-English Lexicon* (Oxford: Clarendon Press, 1996): s.v. "σώζω."
10. Martin Heidegger, *Being and Time*, trans. John Maquarrie (New York: Harper Collins, 2008), 33.
11. *Oxford English Dictionary*, online edition, s.v. *repair*.
12. Gérard Genette, *Narrative Discourse: An Essay in Method*, trans. Jane Lewin (Ithaca, NY: Cornell University Press, 1983), 162.
13. Theodor W. Adorno, *Minima Moralia: Reflections on a Damaged Life*, trans. E. F. N. Jephcott (New York: Verso, 2006), 247.
14. Bruno Latour and Steven Woolgar, *Laboratory Life: The Construction of Scientific Facts*, 2nd ed. (Princeton University Press, 1986), 43–44.
15. See Bruno Latour, *Science in Action: How to Follow Scientists and Engineers Through Society* (Cambridge, MA: Harvard University Press, 1987); Bruno Latour, *Reassembling the Social: An Introduction to Actor-Network-Theory* (Oxford: Oxford University Press, 2005).
16. Steven Shapin, "Following Scientists Around," *Social Studies of Science* 18, no. 3 (August 1988): 538.
17. Michel Foucault, *Le gouvernement de soi et des autres: Cours au Collège de France, 1982–83* (Paris: Gallimard and Seuil, 2008), 7–8.
18. Ibid.: "(1) Un négativisme historicisant puisqu'il s'agit de substituer à une théorie de la connaissance, du pouvoir ou du sujet l'analyse de pratiques historiques déterminées. (2) Un négativisme nominaliste puisqu'il s'agit de substituer à des universaux comme la folie, le crime, la sexualité l'analyse d'expériences qui constituent des formes historiques singulières. (3) Un négativisme à tendance nihiliste, si on étend par là une forme de réflexions qui, au lieu d'indexer des pratiques à des systèmes de valeurs qui permettent de les mesurer, inscrit ces systèmes de valeurs dans le jeu de pratiques arbitraires même si elles sont intelligibles."
19. Michel Foucault, *The Government of Self and Others: Lectures at the Collège de France 1982–1983*, trans. Graham Burchell (New York: Palgrave Macmillan, 2010), 5.
20. Foucault, *Le gouvernement de soi et des autres*, 7: "(1) Ce qui est la question de historicisme: quels ont été les effets et ce que peuvent être les effets de l'analyse historique dans le champ de la pensée historique? (2) Ce qu'est la question du nominalisme: quels ont été les effets de ces critiques nominalistes dans l'analyse des cultures, des connaissances, des institutions, des structures politiques? (3) Ce qu'est la question du nihilisme: qu'ont été et quels peuvent être les effets du nihilisme dans l'acceptation et la transformation des systèmes de valeurs? "
21. Foucault, *Le gouvernement de soi et des autres*, 6: "Aux objections qui postulent la disqualification du nihilisme/nominalismes/historicisme, il faudrait essayer de répondre en faisant une analyse historiciste/nominaliste/nihiliste de ce courant. Et par là je veux dire: non pas édifier dans sa systématicité universelle cette forme de pensée et la justifier en termes de vérité ou de valeur morale, mais chercher à savoir comment a pu se constituer et se développer ce jeu critique, cette forme de pensée" (pp. 7–8).
22. Aristotle, "Posterior Analytics," in *The Basic Works of Aristotle*, ed. Richard McKeon (New York: Random House, 1941), 110.

CHAPTER FOUR

1. Salman Rushdie, *The Satanic Verses: A Novel* (Random House Digital, Inc., 2011), 49.
2. Salman Rushdie, *Midnight's Children: A Novel* (Random House Digital, Inc., 2010), 4.
3. Salman Rushdie, *Shame: A Novel* (Random House Digital, Inc., 2011).
4. For what James D. Faubion has termed the "themitical," see James D. Faubion, *An Anthropology of Ethics* (Cambridge: Cambridge University Press, 2011).
5. John Mitchison interview with Salman Rushdie, "Between God and the Devil," in *Waterstone's Autumn/Winter Catalogue*, reprinted in Pradyumna S. Chauhan, *Salman Rushdie Interviews: A Sourcebook of His Ideas* (Westport, CT: Greenwood Press, 2001), 94.
6. Sail Tripathi and Dina Vakil, "Angels and Devils Are Becoming Confused Ideas," *Indian Post*, September 13, 1987, reprinted in Salman Rushdie and Michael R. Reder, *Conversations With Salman Rushdie* (Jackson: University Press of Mississippi, 2000), 84.
7. Salman Rushdie, *Joseph Anton: A Memoir* (Random House Digital, Inc., 2012), 70.
8. Salman Rushdie, "Between God and Devil," 94.
9. The incident exists in hadith complied by Ibn Ishaq, Waqidi, Ibn Sad, Bukhari, and Tabari:
    "The earliest writer to record the incident around which much controversy has gathered is Ibn Ishaq, the author of the first and most trustworthy biography of the prophet." Michael M. J. Fischer and Mehdi Abedi, "Bombay Talkies, the Word and the World: Salman Rushdie's *Satanic Verses*," *Cultural Anthropology* 5, no. 2 (May 1990): 127. See also, Ibrāhīm Al-Kurānī, "Al-Lum'at al-sanīya fī taḥqīq al-ilqā' fi-1 -umnīya," translation and introduction by Alfred Guillaume, *Bulletin of the School of Oriental and African Studies* 20, no. 1/3, 1937–57 (1957): 291.
10. W. L. Webb, "Salman Rushdie: *Satanic Verses*," in Rushdie and Reder, *Conversations*, 90.
11. Fischer and Abedi, "Bombay Talkies, the Word and the World": 107–59.
12. Al-Kurānī, "Al-Lum'at al-sanīya fī taḥqīq al-ilqā' fi-1 -umnīya," 292: the Naqshbandi Sufi order. Sufis are ascetical mystics, and this order is the only one to trace its lineage to the prophet Mohammad.
13. Rabinow, *Accompaniment*,140–151.
14. Thanks to Joshua Craze, Thomas Hodgman, and Roi Bachmutsky.
15. Yasmine Saleh, "Muslim Leaders Decry Mohammad Cartoons, Urge Peaceful Protest," *Reuters*, September 19, 2012. Webb Keane, "Freedom and Blasphemy: On Indonesian Press Bans and Danish Cartoons," *Public Culture* 21, no. 1 (2009): 47–76. Keane quotes Art Spiegel as describing the work of drawing cartoons as having a "a predisposition toward insult."
16. Esam Mohamed and Maggie Michael, "US Ambassador Killed in Consulate Attack in Libya," *Associated Press*, September 12, 2012. http://bigstory.ap.org/article/us-ambassador-killed-consulate-attack-libya.
17. Michel Foucault, "Polemics, Politics, and Problematizations: An Interview with Michel Foucault," in *The Foucault Reader*, ed. Paul Rabinow (New York: Pantheon, 1984), 382.
18. Foucault, *Hermeneutics of the Subject*, 430.
19. "Chacune de ces figures fournit des appuis ou des formes d'expression de nature différente aux protagonistes. L'identification des modalités de passage d'une configuration ou d'un régime d'épreuve à l'autre peut être opérée à partir d'un ensemble

de traits ou de paramètres." Francis Chateauraynaud and Didier Torny, *Les sombres précurseurs: Une sociologie pragmatique de l'alerte et du risque* (Paris: École des hautes études en sciences sociales, 1999), 70.

20. Madhu Jain, "An Irreverent Journey, " *India Today*, September 15, 1988, reprinted in Lisa Appignanesi and Sara Maitland, *The Rushdie File* (Syracuse, NY: Syracuse University Press, 1989), 38.

21. Ibid.

22. *The Satanic Verses Affair*, BBC documentary, broadcast March 7, 2009.

23. Syed Shahabuddin, "You Did This with Satanic Forethought, Mr. Rushdie," *Times of India*, October 13, 1988, reprinted in *The Rushdie File*, 45–49.

24. Ibid., 48.

25. Rushdie, *Joseph Anton*, 118.

26. Ibid., 119.

27. Ibid.

28. Foucault, "Polemics, Politics, and Problematizations," 382.

29. Jeanne Favret-Saada, "Rushdie et compagnie: Préalables à une anthropologie du blasphème," *Ethnologie française* 22, no. 3 (1992): 251–60.

30. Jeanne Favret-Saada, *Les mots, la mort, les sorts* (Paris: Gallimard, 1977).

31. Bernd Kaussler, *Defending the* Satanic Verses: *Constructive Engagement, British-Iranian Relations and the Right to Freedom of Expression (1989–2004)*, PhD diss., University of St. Andrews, 146.

32. Amir Taheri "Khomeini's Scapegoat," *Times* (London), February 13, 1989.

33. Kaussler, *Defending the Satanic Verses*, 150.

34. Richard Webster, *A Brief History of Blasphemy: Liberalism, Censorship and* The Satanic verses (Oxford: Orwell Press, 1990).

35. Foucault, "Polemics, Politics, and Problematizations," 382.

36. Talal Asad, *Genealogies of Religion: Discipline and Reasons of Power in Christianity and Islam* (Baltimore, MD: Johns Hopkins University Press, 1993), 270.

37. Asad, *Genealogies*, 287.

38. Foucault, "What Is Enlightenment?"; Paul Rabinow, "Modern and Counter-Modern: Ethos and Epoch in Heidegger and Foucault," in ed. Gary Gutting, *The Cambridge Companion to Foucault* (Cambridge: Cambridge University Press, 1994), 247–61.

39. Asad, *Genealogies*, 269.

40. Cf. John H. Zammito, *Kant, Herder, and the Birth of Anthropology* (Chicago: University of Chicago Press, 2002); Edward W. Said, *Culture and Imperialism* (Random House Digital, Inc., 1994).

41. Asad, *Genealogies*, 269.

42. Salman Rushdie to Rajiv Ghandi, *The Rushdie File*, 44.

43. Asad, *Genealogies*, 175.

44. Cf. Lawrence Rosen, "Never in Doubt: Salman Rushdie's Deeper Challenge to Islam," in *The Culture of Islam: Changing Aspects of Contemporary Muslim Life* (Chicago: University of Chicago Press, 2004), 157–174.

45. Rushdie, *Joseph Anton*, 38.

46. Salman Rushdie, *Observer*, January 22, 1989, in *The Rushdie File*, 44.

47. Asad, *Genealogies*, 287.

48. Asad, *Genealogies*, 284.

49. Ibid., 288.

50. Ibid., 19.

51. Fischer and Abedi, "Bombay Talkies," 148.

52. Rushdie, *Joseph Anton*, 272.
53. Salman Rushdie, "Why I Have Embraced Islam," reprinted in *Imaginary Homelands* (London: Penguin, 1991), 430–32.
54. "Rushdie Supporter Says Author No Longer 'Worth Defending,'" January 3, 1991, *Associated Press*.
55. Rushdie's diary entry, January 1, 1990, read in *The Satanic Verses Affair*, BBC documentary, broadcast March 7, 2009.
56. Rushdie, *Joseph Anton*, 274.
57. Ibid., 282.
58. Ibid., 283.
59. Christopher Hitchens, "Siding with Rushdie, " *London Review of Books* 11, no. 20 (October 26, 1989): 11–15.

CHAPTER FIVE

1. Foucault, *Hermeneutics of the Subject*, 466–67. Translation modified. "Que le monde, à travers le bios, soit devenu cette expérience à travers lequel nous nous connaissons nous-même, cet exercice à travers laquelle nous nous connaissons nous-mêmes, cet exercice à travers lequel nous nous nous transformons ou nous nous sauvons, je crois que cela, c'est une transformation, une mutation très importante par rapport à ce qu'était la pensée grecque classique, à savoir que le bios doit être l'objet d'une techn , c'est-à-dire d'un art raisonnable et rationnel." Michel Foucault, *L'herméneutique du sujet, Cours au Collège de France, 1981–82*, 466.
2. Sylvaine Guyot et al., *Racine, ou, L'alchimie du tragique: la Thébaïde, Britannicus, Mithridate* (Paris: Presses Universitaires de France, 2010). In the theater, its emergence constitutes a break with classic tragedy. Scholars have argued convincingly that it is only with the sudden and unexpected collapse of the parameters of pity and fear as the affect poles of tragedy that experimentation with alternatives began to be undertaken. Thus, Racine, the paradigmatic classical tragedian in French theater, introduced pathos into his dramaturgy; its introduction did work to affect his audiences but what they experienced ran against the grain of their expectations, upsetting and confusing them.
3. John Mullan, *Sentiment and Sociability: The Language of Feeling in the Eighteenth Century* (Oxford: Clarendon Press, 1988); G. J. Barker-Benfield, *The Culture of Sensibility: Sex and Society in Eighteenth-Century Britain* (Chicago: University of Chicago Press, 1996); Ian P. Watt, *The Rise of the Novel: Studies in Defoe, Richardson and Fielding* (Berkeley: University of California Press, 2001).
4. F. C. Green, *Diderot's Writings on the Theatre* (Cambridge: Cambridge University Press, 2012).
5. Michel Foucault, *L'herméneutique du sujet*, 467. "Ce défi, c'est celui-ci: comment ce qui se donne comme objet de savoir articulé sur la maitrise de la technē, comment cela peut-il être en même temps le lieu où se manifeste, où s'épreuve et difficilement s'accomplit la vérité du sujet que nous sommes? Comment le monde, qui se donne comme objet de connaissance à partir de la maitrise de la technē, peut-il être en même temps le lieu où s'épreuve le 'soi-même' comme sujet éthique de la vérité?"
6. Hubertus Butin, *Editions*, me Collections room (Berlin, 2012), http://www.gerhard-richter.com/videos/exhibitions-1/gerhard-richter-editions-55.
7. For example, Reinhard Spieler, ed., *Gerhard Richter: Ohne Farbe / Without Color* (Ostfildern-Ruit, Germany: Hatje Cantz, 2005).

8. Aline Guillermet, Tate, video (17 minutes and 19 seconds), http://www.gerhard -richter.com/videos/talks-3/chance-process-and-chance-effects-51.

9. Butin, *Editions* (31 minutes, 4 seconds).

10. "Interview with Jan Thorn-Prikker on the work WAR CUT," First published: Jan Thorn-Prikker, "Gerhard Richter im Gesprach mit Jan Thorn-Prikker," in *Gerhard Richter im Albertium*, exhib. Cat. *Galerie Neue Meister*, Dresden, 2004, 74–88, translated by Ben Posener. Reproduced in Gerhard Richter, Dietmar Elger, and Hans-Ulrich Obrist, *Gerhard Richter: Writings 1961–2007* (New York: D.A.P./Distributed Art Publishers, 2009), 463.

11. Robert Storr, *September: A History Painting by Gerhard Richter* (London: Tate, 2010).

12. "Interview with Jan Thorn-Prikker," 462.

13. Ibid., 463.

14. Ibid., 463.

15. Rabinow, *Marking Time*, 2.

16. Mark Godfrey, "Damaged Landscapes," in *Gerhard Richter: Panorama, a Retrospective*, ed. Mark Godfrey, Nicholas Serota, and Achim Burchardt-Hume (London: Tate Publishing, 2011).

17. Godfrey, "Damaged Landscapes," 81.

18. Ibid., 83.

19. Ibid., 83.

20. Ibid., 86.

21. Godfrey, Ibid., 87.

22. Joris Karl Huysmans, *Against Nature*, trans. Margaret Mauldon (Oxford: Oxford University Press, 1998); Charles Baudelaire, *The Painter of Modern Life and Other Essays*, trans. and ed. Jonathan Mayne (London: Phaidon Press, 1995).

23. Interview with Benjamin H. D. Buchloh 1986, in *Gerhard Richter Writings*, 163–87.

24. Rosalind E. Krauss, *The Optical Unconscious* (Cambridge, MA: MIT Press, 1994), 254–56.

25. Georges Didi-Huberman, *Images in Spite of All* (Chicago: University of Chicago Press, 2008) (original, *Images malgé tout* [Paris: Les Editions de Minuit, 2003]).

26. Michel Foucault, *Le gouvernement de soi et des autres, Cours au Collège de France, 1982–83* (Paris: Gallimard and Seuil, 2008), 7: "Reproches, c'est-à-dire les objections qui sont telles qu'à s'en défendre on souscrit fatalement à ce qu'elles soutiennent."

27. "Eric Clapton's Richter Sets a Record Price for any Living Artist at Auction," *On Camera, Sotheby's*, October 16, 2012.

28. Nicholas Kulish, "Germans Embrace Artist as Home Grown Hero," *New York Times*, February 19, 2012.

29. Gerhard Richter, in *Gerhard Richter, Writings 1961–2007* (New York: D.A.P., 2009), "Notes, 1989," 212.

30. Ibid., 245–46.

31. Ibid., "Interview with Benjamin H. D. Buchloh, 1986," 177–78.

32. Ibid., "Interview with Benjamin H. D. Buchloh, 2004," 494–95.

CONCLUSION

1. Foucault, *Hermeneutics of the Subject*, 485–86.

2. Adorno, *Minima Moralia*, 126.

3. Ibid.

4. Ibid.

5. We consulted Martin Jay, the world's leading expert on the Frankfurt school, as to a possible referent and he did not know of one.
6. Adorno, *Minima Moralia*, 127.
7. Ibid.

TERMS OF ENGAGEMENT

1. John Dewey, *How We Think* (Boston: D. C. Heath & Co., 1910), 1–13.
2. Liddell and Scott, *Greek-English Lexicon*: s.v. ἀγών, ὁ.
3. Deleuze and Guattari, *What Is Philosophy?*, 4–9.
4. Michel Foucault, *The Order of Things: An Archaeology of the Human Sciences* (London: Tavistock Publications, 1966), 219–21.
5. Liddell and Scott, *Greek-English Lexicon*, S.v ἄσκησις, ἡ.
6. Michel Foucault, *The History of Sexuality*, vol. 2: *The Use of Pleasure* (New York: Vintage, 1990), 9.
7. Liddell and Scott, *Greek-English Lexicon*, S.v ἀταραξία, ἡ.
8. Foucault, "What Is Enlightenment?," 34.
9. Nietzsche's use of the term is best known in his *Unzeitgemässe Betrachtungen (Untimely Observations)*. Mit einem Nachwort von Ralph-Rainer Wuthenow (Insel Verlag, 1981).
10. Paul Rabinow, "Foucault's Untimely Struggle: Toward a Form of Spirituality," *Theory Culture Society* 25, no. 6 (2009): 27.
11. Rabinow and Bennett, *Designing Human Practices*, 179.
12. Liddell and Scott *Greek-English Lexicon*: s.v. βίος, ὁ.
13. Rabinow, *Marking Time*, 2.
14. Dewey, *Essays in Experimental Logic*, 11.
15. Foucault, *Hermeneutics of the Subject*, 322.
16. Paul Rabinow and Gaymon Bennett, *Contemporary Equipment: A Diagnostic* (ARC Ebook, 2012), 6.
17. Foucault, *History of Sexuality*, 2:26.
18. Bios-Technika, *Form*, http://bios-technika.net/concepts.php#form.
19. Foucault, *Le gouvernement de soi et des autres*, 4–5.
20. Fredric Jameson, *Brecht on Method* (New York: Verso, 1998), 21–36.
21. Liddell and Scott *Greek-English Lexicon*: s.v. ὅρος, ὁ.
22. Aristotle, *Nicomachean Ethics*.
23. John Dewey, "Propositions, Warranted Assertibility, and Truth," *Journal of Philosophy* 38, no. 7 (1941): 180.
24. Liddell and Scott, *Greek-English Lexicon*: s.v. καιρός, ὁ.
25. Liddell and Scott, *Greek-English Lexicon*: s.v λῆψις, ἡ.
26. Liddell and Scott, *Greek-English Lexicon*: s.v μετάληψις, ἡ.
27. Harold Bloom, "Poetry, Revisionism, Repression," *Critical Inquiry* 2, no. 2 (Winter 1975): 246.
28. Rabinow and Bennett, *Contemporary Equipment*, 27.
29. Ibid., 52–53.
30. Genette, *Narrative Discourse*, 162.
31. Liddell and Scott, *Greek-English Lexicon*: s.v. παρρησία, ἡ.
32. Foucault, *Government of the Self and Others*.
33. Rabinow and Bennett, *Designing Human Practices*, 179.
34. Liddell and Scott, *Greek-English Lexicon*: s.v. φιλία, ἡ.
35. Foucault, *Hermeneutics of the Subject*, 183.

36. Lewis and Short, *Latin Dictionary*: s.v. *stultītĭa, ae*, f. *stultus.*
37. Foucault, *Hermeneutics of the Subject*, 131–33.
38. Liddell and Scott *Greek-English Lexicon*: s.v. τέχνη, ἡ.
39. Rabinow and Bennett, *Contemporary Equipment*, 44.
40. Lewis and Short, *Latin Dictionary*: s.v. *vindicare.*
41. Dewey, "Propositions, Warranted Assertibility, and Truth," 172.

BIBLIOGRAPHY

Adorno, Theodor W. *Minima Moralia: Reflections on a Damaged Life*. Translated by E. F. N. Jephcott. New York: Verso, 2006.

Agamben, Giorgio. *Homo Sacer: Sovereign Power and Bare Life*. Palo Alto, CA: Stanford University Press, 1998.

———. *The Positivist Dispute in German Sociology*. London: Heinemann, 1976.

Al-Kurānī, Ibrāhīm. "Al-Lum'at Al-Sanīya Fī Taḥqīq Al-Ilqā' Fi-L-Umnīya." Translation and introduction by Alfred Guillaume. *Bulletin of the School of Oriental and African Studies* 20, no. 1/3 (1957): 291–303.

Allison, June. *Power and Preparedness in Thucydides*. Baltimore, MD: Johns Hopkins University Press, 1989.

Appignanesi, Lisa, and Sara Maitland. *The Rushdie File*. Syracuse, NY: Syracuse University Press, 1989.

Aristotle. *Nicomachean Ethics*. Translated by Harris Rackham. Cambridge, MA: Harvard University Press (Loeb Classical Library), 1934.

———. "Posterior Analytics." In *The Basic Works of Aristotle*, edited by Richard McKeon. New York: Random House, 1941.

Asad, Talal. *Genealogies of Religion: Discipline and Reasons of Power in Christianity and Islam*. Baltimore, MD: Johns Hopkins University Press, 1993.

Barker-Benfield, G. J. *The Culture of Sensibility: Sex and Society in Eighteenth-Century Britain*. Chicago: University of Chicago Press, 1996.

Bartlett, Robert C, and Susan D. Collins, trans. *Aristotle's Nicomachean Ethics*. Chicago: University of Chicago Press, 2011.

Baudelaire, Charles. *The Painter of Modern Life and Other Essays*. Translated and edited by Jonathan Mayne. London: Phaidon Press, 1995.

Bellah, Robert N., et al. *Habits of the Heart: Individualism and Commitment in American Life*. Berkeley: University of California Press, 1985.

Bios-Technika. *Form*. http://bios-technika.net/concepts.php#form.

Bloom, Harold. "Poetry, Revisionism, Repression." *Critical Inquiry* 2, no. 2 (Winter 1975).

Blumenberg, Hans. "'Imitation of Nature': Toward a Prehistory of the Idea of the Creative Being." *Qui Parle* 12, no. 1 (Spring/Summer 2000): 17–54.

———. *The Legitimacy of the Modern Age*, translated and edited by Robert M. Wallace. Cambridge, MA: MIT Press, 1985.

———. *Paradigms for a Metaphorology*. Ithaca, NY: Cornell University Press, 2010.

Bourdieu, Pierre. *Outline of a Theory of Practice*. Cambridge: Cambridge University Press, 1977.

Burke, Tom. *Dewey's New Logic: A Reply to Russell*. Chicago: University of Chicago Press, 1998.

Butin, Hubertus. *Editions*, me Collections room. Berlin, 2012. http://www.gerhard-richter.com/videos/exhibitions-1/gerhard-richter-editions-55.

Caygill, Howard. *A Kant Dictionary*. Oxford: John Wiley & Sons, 1995.

Chateauraynaud, Francis, and Didier Torny. *Les sombres précurseurs: Une sociologie pragmatique de l'alerte et du risque* (Paris: École des hautes études en sciences sociales, 1999).

Chauhan, Pradyumna S. *Salman Rushdie Interviews: A Sourcebook of His Ideas*. Westport, CT: Greenwood Press, 2001.

Cooper, John M, and J. F. Procopé, eds. and trans. *Seneca: Moral and Political Essays*. Cambridge: Cambridge University Press, 2006.

Deleuze, Gilles. *Foucault*. Paris: Éditions de Minuit, 2004.

———. *Kant's Critical Philosophy: The Doctrine of the Faculties*. London: Athlone, 1984.

———. *Nietzsche and Philosophy*. New York: Continuum, 1986.

Deleuze, Gilles, and Félix Guattari. *Kafka: Toward a Minor Literature*. Minneapolis: University of Minnesota Press, 2004.

———. *What Is Philosophy?* New York: Columbia University Press, 1996.

Dewey, John. *Essays in Experimental Logic*. Chicago: University of Chicago Press, 1916; rep. New York: Dover, 2004.

———. *How We Think*. Boston: D. C. Heath & Co., 1910.

———. *Logic: The Theory of Inquiry*. New York: Henry Holt, 1938.

———. "Propositions, Warranted Assertibility, and Truth." *Journal of Philosophy* 38, no. 7 (1941): 169–86.

———. *The Public and Its Problems*. New York: Henry Holt, 1927.

———. *Reconstruction in Philosophy*. Enlarged edition. Boston: Beacon Press, 1948.

Didi-Huberman, Georges. *Images in Spite of All*. Chicago: University of Chicago Press, 2008.

Diogo, Sardinha. "De Livres considérés à tort comme mineurs." *Rue Descartes*, no. 75 (2012/2013): 1–5.

Djaballah, Marc. *Kant, Foucault, and Forms of Experience*. New York: Routledge, 2011.

"Eric Clapton's Richter Sets a Record Price for Any Living Artist at Auction." *On Camera, Sotheby's*. June 16, 2012.

Faubion, James D. *An Anthropology of Ethics*. Cambridge: Cambridge University Press, 2011.

———. *Modern Greek Lessons: A Primer in Historical Constructivism*. Princeton, NJ: Princeton University Press, 1995.

Favret-Saada, Jeanne. *Les mots, la mort, les sorts*. Paris: Gallimard, 1977.

———. "Rushdie et compagnie: Préalables à une anthropologie du blasphème." *Ethnologie française* 22, no. 3 (1992): 251–60.

Fischer, Michael M. J., and Mehdi Abedi. "Bombay Talkies, the Word and the World: Salman Rushdie's *Satanic Verses*." *Cultural Anthropology* 5, no. 2 (May 1990): 107–59.

———. *An Anthropology of Ethics*. Cambridge: Cambridge University Press, 2011.

Foucault, Michel. *The Courage of Truth: The Government of Self and Others II; Lectures at the Collège de France, 1983–1984*. New York: Palgrave Macmillan, 2011.

———. *The Foucault Reader*. Edited by Paul Rabinow. New York: Pantheon, 1984.

————. *Le gouvernement de soi et des autres: Cours au Collège de France, 1982–1983*. Paris: Seuil and Gallimard, 2008.

————. *The Government of Self and Others: Lectures at the Collège de France 1982–1983*. Translated by Graham Burchell. New York: Palgrave Macmillan, 2010.

————. *The Hermeneutics of the Subject: Lectures at the Collège de France 1981–1982*. Translated by Graham Burchell. New York: Palgrave Macmillan, 2005.

————. *L'hermeneutique du suject, Cours au Collège de France, 1981–1982*. Paris: Seuil and Gallimard, 2001.

————. *The History of Sexuality*. Vol. 2, *The Use of Pleasure*. New York: Vintage, 1990.

————. *Introduction to Kant's Anthropology*. Translated by Kate Briggs and Robert Nigro. Los Angeles, CA: Semiotext(e), 2008.

————. "Omnes et Singulatim: Towards a Critique of Political Reason." In *Power: Essential Works of Foucault: 1954–1984*, edited by James D. Faubion, 298–325. New York: New Press, 2000.

————. "On the Genealogy of Ethics: Overview of Work in Progress." In *The Foucault Reader*, edited by Paul Rabinow, 340–72. New York: Pantheon, 1984. [OR In *Beyond Structuralism and Hermeneutics*. Chicago: The University of Chicago Press, 1983.

————. *The Order of Things: An Archaeology of the Human Sciences*. London: Tavistock Publications, 1996.

————. "Qu'est-ce que les lumières?" In *Dits et écrits*, vol. 1, no. 2: 1381–97. Paris: Gallimard, 2001.

————. "Table ronde du 20 Mai 1978." In *Dits et Écrits*, vol. 2. Paris: Gallimard, 2001.

————. "What Is Enlightenment?" In *The Foucault Reader*, edited by Paul Rabinow, 32–50. New York: Pantheon Books, 1984.

Geertz, Clifford. "Ideology as a Cultural System." In *The Interpretation of Cultures*. New York: Basic Books, 1973.

————. "Thinking as a Moral Act: Ethical Dimensions of Anthropological Fieldwork in the New States." *Antioch Review* 28, no. 2 (1968): 34–59.

Genette, Gérard. *Narrative Discourse: An Essay in Method*. Translated by Jane E. Lewin. Ithaca, NY: Cornell University Press, 1983.

Godfrey, Mark, Nicholas Serota, and Achim Borchardt-Hume, eds. *Gerhard Richter: Panorama, a Retrospective*. London: Tate Publishing, 2011.

Green, F. C. *Diderot's Writings on the Theatre*. Cambridge: Cambridge University Press, 2012.

Guyot, Sylvaine, et al. *Racine, ou, L'alchimie du tragique: La Thébaïde, Britannicus, Mithridate*. Paris: Presses Universitaires de France, 2010.

Haan, Norma, et al. *Social Science as Moral Inquiry*. New York: Columbia University Press, 1983.

Heidegger, Martin. "The Age of the World Picture." In *Heidegger: Off the Beaten Track*, translated and edited by Julian Young and Kenneth Haynes. Cambridge: Cambridge University Press, 2002.

————. *Being and Time*. Translated by John Maquarrie. New York: Harper Collins, 2008.

Hirschman, Albert O. *Exit, Voice, and Loyalty: Responses to Decline in Firms, Organizations, and States*. Cambridge, MA: Harvard University Press, 1970.

Hitchens, Christopher. "Siding with Rushdie." *London Review of Books* 11, no. 20 (October 26, 1989): 11–15.

Huysmans, Joris Karl. *Against Nature*. Translated by Margaret Mauldon. Oxford: Oxford University Press, 1998.

Jameson, Frederic. *Brecht on Method*. New York: Verso, 1998.

Kant, Immanuel. *Anthropology from a Pragmatic Point of View*. Cambridge: Cambridge University Press, 2006.

———. "Idea for a Universal History with a Cosmopolitan Aim." Translated by Allen W. Wood. In Immanuel Kant, *Anthropology, History, and Education*, translated by Robert B. Louden and Günter Zöller. Cambridge: Cambridge University Press, 2008.

———. *Lectures on Anthropology*. Translated by Robert B. Louden et al. Cambridge: Cambridge University Press, 2013.

Kant, Immanuel, and Michel Foucault. *Anthropologie du point de vue pragmatique et introduction à l'Anthropologie*. Paris: Vrin, 2008.

Kaussler, Bernd. *Defending the* Satanic Verses*: Constructive Engagement, British-Iranian Relations and the Right to Freedom of Expression (1989–2004)*. PhD diss., University of St. Andrews, 2008.

Keane, Webb. "Freedom and Blasphemy: On Indonesian Press Bans and Danish Cartoons." *Public Culture* 21, no. 1 (2009): 47–76.

Ker, James. *The Deaths of Seneca*. Oxford: Oxford University Press, 2009.

———. *Nocturnal Letters: Roman Temporal Practices and Seneca's Epistulae Morales*. Diss., Univ. of California–Berkeley, 2002.

Krauss, Rosalind E. *The Optical Unconscious*. Cambridge, MA: MIT Press, 1994.

Kulish, Nicholas. "Germans Embrace Artist as Home Grown Hero." *New York Times*. February 19, 2012.

Latour, Bruno. "An Attempt at a Compositionist Manifesto." *New Literary History* 41, no. 3 (Summer 2010).

———. *Reassembling the Social: An Introduction to Actor-Network-Theory*. Oxford: Oxford University Press, 2005.

———. *Science in Action: How to Follow Scientists and Engineers through Society*. Cambridge, MA: Harvard University Press, 1987.

Latour, Bruno, and Steven Woolgar. *Laboratory Life: The Construction of Scientific Facts*. 2nd ed. Princeton, NJ: Princeton University Press, 1986.

Lewis, Charlton T., and Charles Short. *A Latin Dictionary*. Oxford: Oxford University Press, 1956.

Liddell, Henry George, and Robert Scott. *A Greek-English Lexicon*. Oxford: Clarendon Press, 1996.

Lienhardt, Godfrey. "Modes of Thought in Primitive Society." *New Blackfriars* 34, no. 399 (June 1953): 269–77.

Long, George, trans. *Meditations of the Emperor Marcus Aurelius Antoninus*. London: Chesterfield Society, n.d.

Luhmann, Niklas. *Observations on Modernity*. Translated by William Whobrey. Palo Alto, CA: Stanford University Press, 1998.

Macintyre, Alisdair. *After Virtue: A Study in Moral Theory*. Notre Dame, IN: University of Notre Dame Press. 2nd ed., 1984.

Marcus, George, E., and James Clifford, eds. *Writing Culture: The Poetics and Politics of Ethnography*. Berkeley: University of California Press, 1986.

Marcus, George E., and Michael M. J. Fischer. *Anthropology as Cultural Critique: An Experimental Moment in the Human Sciences*. Chicago: University of Chicago Press, 1986.

Mohamed, Esam, and Maggie Michael. "US Ambassador Killed in Consulate Attack in Libya." *Associated Press*. September 12, 2012. http://bigstory.ap.org/article/us-ambassador-killed-consulate-attack-libya.

Mullan, John. *Sentiment and Sociability: The Language of Feeling in the Eighteenth Century.* Oxford: Clarendon Press, 1988.

Nietzsche, Friedrich. *Unzeitgemässe Betrachtungen [Untimely Observations].* Mit einem Nachwort von Ralph-Rainer Wuthenow. Insel Verlag, 1981.

Ong, Aihwa, and Stephen J. Collier. *Global Assemblages: Technology, Politics, and Ethics as Anthropological Problems.* Oxford: Wiley, 2004.

Rabinow, Paul. *The Accompaniment: Assembling the Contemporary.* Chicago: University of Chicago Press, 2011.

———. *Anthropos Today: Reflections on Modern Equipment.* Princeton, NJ: Princeton University Press, 2003.

———. "Beyond Ethnography: Anthropology as Nominalism." *Cultural Anthropology* 3, no. 4 (1988): 355–64.

———. "How to Submit to Inquiry: Dewey and Foucault." *Pluralist* 7, no. 3 (2012).

———. *Marking Time: On the Anthropology of the Contemporary.* Princeton, NJ: Princeton University Press, 2007.

———. "Modern and Counter-Modern: Ethos and Epoch in Heidegger and Foucault." In *The Cambridge Companion to Foucault,* edited by Gary Gutting, 247–61. Cambridge: Cambridge University Press, 1994.

———. "Prosperity, Amelioration, Flourishing: From a Logic of Practical Judgment to Reconstruction." *Journal of Law and Literature* 21, no. 3 (2009): 301–20.

———. *Reflections on Fieldwork in Morocco.* Berkeley: University of California Press, 1977.

———. *Symbolic Domination: Cultural Form and Historical Change in Morocco.* Chicago: University of Chicago Press, 1975.

Rabinow, Paul, et al. *Designs for an Anthropology of the Contemporary.* Durham, NC: Duke University Press, 2008.

Rabinow, Paul, and Gaymon Bennett. *Contemporary Equipment: A Diagnostic.* ARC e-book, 2012.

———. *Designing Human Practices: An Experiment with Synthetic Biology.* Chicago: University of Chicago Press, 2012.

———. "A Diagnostic of Equipmental Platforms." *ARC Working Paper,* no. 9 (2007).

———. "Foucault's Untimely Struggle: Toward a Form of Spirituality." *Theory Culture Society* 25, no. 6 (2009).

———. "From Bioethics to Human Practices, or Assembling Contemporary Equipment." In *Tactical Biopolitics Art, Activism, and Technoscience,* edited by Beatriz Da Costa and Kavita Philips, 389–99. Cambridge, MA: MIT Press, 2007.

———. "Human Practices: Interfacing Three Modes of Collaboration." In *The Ethics of Protocells: Moral and Social Implications of Creating Life in the Laboratory,* edited by Mark A. Bedau and Emily C. Parke, 263–90. Cambridge, MA: MIT Press, 2008.

———. "Introduction: The History of Systems of Thought." In *Essential Works of Foucault (1954–1984),* vol. 1: *Ethics,* edited by Paul Rabinow. New York: New Press, 1994.

———. "Synthetic Biology: Ethical Ramifications." *Journal of Systems and Synthetic Biology* 3, no. 1 (2009): 99–108.

Rabinow, Paul, Gaymon Bennett, and Anthony Stavrianakis. "Reply to the Respondents." *Journal of Law and Literature* 21, no. 3 (2009): 471–79.

Rabinow, Paul, Andrew Lakoff, and Stephen Collier. "Biosecurity: Towards an Anthropology of the Contemporary." *Anthropology Today* 20, no. 5 (October 2004): 3–7.

Rabinow, Paul, and Anthony Stavrianakis. *Contemporary Equipment: A Diagnostic.* ARC e-book, 2012.

———. *Demands of the Day: On the Logic of Anthropological Inquiry.* Chicago: Chicago University Press, 2013.

Rackham, Harris, trans. *Aristotle: Nicomachean Ethics.* Cambridge, MA: Loeb Classical Library, 1934.

Reiss, Hans, ed. *Kant: Political Writings.* Translated by H. B. Nisbet. Cambridge: Cambridge University Press, 2001.

Rheinberger, Hans-Jorg. *Towards a History of Epistemic Things: Synthesizing Proteins in the Test Tube.* Palo Alto, CA: Stanford University Press, 1997.

Richter, Gerhard, Dietmar Elger, and Hans-Ulrich Obrist. *Gerhard Richter: Writings 1961–2007.* New York: D.A.P./Distributed Art Publishers, 2009.

Rose, Nikolas. *The Politics of Life Itself: Biomedicine, Power, and Subjectivity in the Twenty-First Century.* Princeton, NJ: Princeton University Press, 2006.

Rushdie, Salman. *Joseph Anton: A Memoir.* Random House Digital, Inc., 2012.

———. *Midnight's Children: A Novel.* Random House Digital, Inc., 2010.

———. *The Satanic Verses: A Novel.* Random House Digital, Inc., 2011.

———. *Shame: A Novel.* Random House Digital, Inc., 2011.

Rushdie, Salman, and Michael R. Reder. *Conversations with Salman Rushdie.* Jackson: University Press of Mississippi, 2000.

"Rushdie Supporter Says Author No Longer 'Worth Defending,' " January 3, 1991, *Associated Press.*

Said, Edward W. *Culture and Imperialism.* Random House Digital, Inc., 1994.

Saleh, Yasmine. "Muslim Leaders Decry Mohammad Cartoons, Urge Peaceful Protest." *Reuters.* September 19, 2012.

The Satanic Verses Affair. BBC documentary. Broadcast March 7, 2009.

Seneca. *On the Tranquility of Mind.* In *Dialogues and Essays.* Translated by John Davie. New York: Oxford University Press, 2009.

Shahabuddin, Syed. "You Did This with Satanic Forethought, Mr. Rushdie." *Times of India.* October 13, 1988; reprinted in Appignanesi and Maitland, *Rushdie File*, 45–49.

Shapin, Steven. "Following Scientists Around." *Social Studies of Science* 18, no. 3 (August 1988): 533–50.

Spieler, Reinhard, ed., *Gerhard Richter: Ohne Farbe / Without Color.* Ostfildern-Ruit, Germany: Hatje Cantz, 2005.

Storr, Robert. *September: A History Painting by Gerhard Richter.* London: Tate, 2010.

Taheri, Amir. "Khomeini's Scapegoat." *Times* (London). February 13, 1989.

Volbers, Jörg. "Michel Foucault, philosophe de la liberté? Sur sa lecture de Kant dans l'introduction à l'anthropologie." *Rue Descartes*, no. 75 (2012/2013).

Watt, Ian P. *The Rise of the Novel: Studies in Defoe, Richardson and Fielding.* Berkeley: University of California Press, 2001.

Weber, Max. *From Max Weber: Essays in Sociology.* Edited by Hans Gerth and C. Wright Mills. Oxford: Oxford University Press, 1946.

———. *The Methodology of Social Sciences.* Translated and edited by Edward Shils and Henry Finch. Glencoe, IL: Free Press, 1949.

———. *The Protestant Ethic and the Spirit of Capitalism.* New York: Scribner, 1958.

Webster, Richard. *A Brief History of Blasphemy: Liberalism, Censorship and* The Satanic Verses. Orwell Press, 1990.

Zammito, John H. *Kant, Herder, and the Birth of Anthropology.* Chicago: University of Chicago Press, 2002.

INDEX

www.ingramcontent.com/pod-product-compliance
Lightning Source LLC
Chambersburg PA
CBHW032138020426
42334CB00016B/1209